Prescriptions FOR A WOMAN'S Soul

BRENDA ROLLINS, ED.D.

D1501016

Publishing Designs, Inc.

Publishing Designs, Inc.
P.O. Box 3241
Huntsville, Alabama 35810

All scripture quotations, unless otherwise indicated, are taken
from the King James Version.

Publisher's Cataloging-in-Publication Data

Rollins, Brenda Vance, 1950—
Prescription for a Woman's Soul / Brenda Vance Rollins
1. Biblical Teaching 2. Christian Maturity 3. Christian Women—Religious
Life.
I. Title.
ISBN 978-0-929540-71-9
248.8

Printed in the United States of America

DEDICATION

With all my love to my mother Jean Grant Vance, who first gave me physical life and then taught me about eternal life, and to my husband Tom Rollins, my partner for life in Jesus Christ. "Love never fails" (1 Corinthians 13:13).

CONTENTS

PREFACE

I have always enjoyed creating and teaching Bible lessons for ladies' classes of all ages. This workbook was written with a desire to continue to make my "calling and election sure" and to spotlight some of the biblical women who are outstanding examples of the qualities Peter listed (2 Peter 1:5–11). I pray that this small book will assist you in your diligent effort to live a Christian life. May God bless and keep you all.

INTRODUCTION

The apostle Peter most likely wrote this letter very late in his life. The days of his impetuous spirit and hair-trigger temper were long gone. He had personally witnessed his Savior's being brutally crucified by the Romans. He had lived many years haunted by the memory of his own denial of Christ.

Yes, Peter was all of these things when he wrote the book of 2 Peter, but he was much more. He was a man who had raised the dead (Acts 9:40), preached the good news of Jesus Christ and Him crucified to a countless multitude (Acts 2), established churches, and proclaimed to thousands the gospel of Christ as the key to eternal life.

It is here, at the end of his life, that we can picture Peter as a kind of "soul physician" writing prescriptions for Christ's disciples of the first century and for all Christians yet to come. But instead of prescribing medicines to promote physical health, his prescriptions promoted spiritual health, assuring participants an entrance "into the everlasting kingdom of our Lord and Savior Jesus Christ."

We women often find ourselves in the role of physical caretakers who must be especially receptive to physicians' instructions. But who is our spiritual caretaker? *Prescriptions for a Woman's Soul* is designed as a spiritual guide from this seasoned apostle. In short, Peter prescribes not only the foundation of faith, but he also gives additional "prescriptions" to make us fit for the church—the kingdom of heaven.

What are our objectives for these lessons?

୧୭ Define each quality prescribed by Peter.

୧୭ Search the Bible to find out how we can acquire each characteristic.

ℰ Examine the lives of women in the Bible who possessed each attribute.

The entire book is based on 2 Peter 1:5–11:

> And beside this, giving all diligence, add to your faith virtue; and to virtue knowledge; and to knowledge temperance; and to temperance patience; and to patience godliness; and to godliness brotherly kindness; and to brotherly kindness charity. For if these things be in you, and abound, they make you that ye shall neither be barren nor unfruitful in the knowledge of our Lord Jesus Christ. But he that lacketh these things is blind, and cannot see afar off, and hath forgotten that he was purged from his old sins. Wherefore the rather, brethren, give diligence to make your calling and election sure: for if ye do these things, ye shall never fall: for so an entrance shall be ministered unto you abundantly into the everlasting kingdom of our Lord and Savior Jesus Christ.

So come, let us begin our study of *Prescriptions for a Woman's Soul.*

Chapter 1

Faith

The Foundation

Prescription

And beside this, giving all diligence, add to your faith *virtue; and to virtue knowledge; and to knowledge temperance; and to temperance patience; and to patience godliness; and to godliness brotherly kindness; and to brotherly kindness charity* (2 Peter 1:5–7).

Physician's Instructions

Blessed is the man [or woman] that trusteth in the Lord, and whose hope the Lord is (Jeremiah 17:7).

Daily Dose

Hebrews 11:1	Hebrews 11:6
1 Corinthians 11:1	Romans 12:3

Matthew 17:19–20

What Is Faith?

Peter's first "soul prescription" instructs us to "add to your faith" all the godly attributes that follow. Since we know that faith is to be our foundation, it is extremely important that we understand what faith really is. The Scriptures say, "Faith is the substance of things hoped for, the evidence of things not seen" (Hebrews 11:1). This passage uses a legal term, "evidence," to explain faith. Evidence is something offered as proof of certain facts. Faith is our proof of heaven and all the other "things not seen."

Hebrews 11:6 gives us further reasons for defining and seeking faith: "But without faith it is impossible to please him: for he that cometh to God must believe that he is, and that he is a rewarder of them that diligently seek him." You must desire to please God, otherwise, why would you be studying this book? Since we can't be pleasing if we lack faith, then it is our duty to own it and to add to it the other graces that Peter describes.

OUR CHRISTIAN FAITH MUST BE FED AND CHERISHED.

It is clear that having a genuine faith in God is the first condition of our salvation. The only way we will ever be in the presence of God in heaven is to become like His Son, Jesus Christ. If we hope to imitate Christ as Paul instructed (1Corinthians 11:1 ASV) it is necessary for us to add each of Peter's prescriptions to our own characters.

Just as a pediatrician's list for a young mother includes things that will help her baby grow up strong and whole, Peter's list describes specific qualities we Christian women should add to our faith in order to make our "calling and election sure" (2 Peter 1:10). In short, when we start to follow his directions, we are well on the way to becoming mature, whole Christians.

Our faith can grow. Paul commended the Christians in Thessalonica, "because your faith groweth exceedingly" (2 Thessalonians 1:3). But be careful. Our faith can also decrease. Jesus reprimanded His disciples when their faith faltered: "O ye of little faith" (Matthew 6:30). Peter acknowledged that faith can fluctuate when he said we should be "giving all diligence" to keep adding on to our existing good character. The entire growth process helps us understand "what manner of persons" we ought to be (2 Peter 3:11).

Look again at our "Prescription" text. Peter emphasizes that faith is to be nurtured. Just as a baby grows strong by eating nourishing foods and getting lots of rest and exercise, women become stronger Christians by acquiring virtue, knowledge, and all the other qualities Peter lists. As a baby must be cared for and loved, so our Christian faith must be fed and cherished. If faith the size of a mustard seed can move mountains, just imagine what a strong, mature faith made up of all these qualities can do!

> And Jesus said unto them . . . Verily I say unto you, if ye have faith as a grain of mustard seed, ye shall say unto this mountain, Remove hence to yonder place; and it shall remove; and nothing shall be impossible unto you (Matthew 17:20).

Don't you want to strive for this type of faith?

How Can I Live By Faith?

The seedlings of true faith are planted each time a person hears the gospel taught by a knowledgeable servant of God.

> How then shall they call on him in whom they have not believed? and how shall they believe in him of whom they have not heard? and how shall they hear without a preacher? And how shall they preach, except they be sent? as it is written, How beautiful are the feet of them that preach the gospel of peace, and bring glad tidings of good things! But they have not all obeyed the gospel. For Esaias saith, Lord, who hath believed our report? So then faith cometh by hearing, and hearing by the word of God (Romans 10:14).

The Scriptures tell us:

ℰℽ The just shall live by faith (Habakkuk 2:4).

ℰℽ Faith can make us whole (Matthew 9:22; Mark 5:34).

ℰℽ Faith can save us (Luke 7:50).

ℰℽ Christians are to "walk by faith, not by sight" (2 Corinthians 5:7).

Certainly, these and other passages convince us that the foundation of our Christian character must be faith.

How can we develop the kind of sustaining faith that will see us through until Judgment Day? What can Christian girls or women do to strengthen their foundations of faith? Consider the following:

1. *Listen to the Word of God as often as possible.* Romans 10:17 tells us that "faith cometh by hearing," and Proverbs 4:20–22 cautions us to keep the Word in the midst of our hearts. *Listen* means to understand and to react to what you hear or read. Think about what you read in the Bible. Talk about it with your family members and friends. Reflect on it. Decide what place the scriptural teachings will have in your daily life. Make a conscious decision to hear the Word proclaimed publicly as often as possible. Invite others to hear it with you. Use all the technological devices you have in order to listen to the Bible being read, sermons being preached, and scriptural songs being sung.

What we listen to affects what we believe. The television is a marvelous invention, but it often takes the place of activities that enable us to hear the Word of God. Why not use it to watch and listen to the godly programs which are becoming more numerous each year? If you aren't sure where to find these kinds of programs, ask your minister, an elder, or a close Christian friend for advice. You might be surprised at the variety that exists. Use your computer to read articles written by ministers and other members of the Lord's church all over this country. Use your CD player or MP3 player to listen to scriptural a cappella singing groups. By doing these things you can optimize your opportunities to listen to the Word of God as often as possible.

2. *Obey God in your daily activities.* In Acts 5:29, Peter and the other apostles stated, "We ought to obey God rather than men." After all, we have the world's best book to guide us in exercising our spiritual muscles. Faith grows stronger with use, so use it as often as possible in your daily interactions with others. We women are not hesitant to tell a neighbor or even a stranger about a sale at the local grocery or a remedy for some ailment. Why not mention the cure for the soul? Today might be the best time to invite a neighbor for

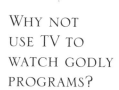

WHY NOT USE TV TO WATCH GODLY PROGRAMS?

coffee or tea, along with a private Bible study at your table! Not only should Christian women take time everyday to communicate with God through prayer and study, they should choose to obey God's teachings through their daily relations with others.

3. *Always be thankful.* Paul reminds us, "In every thing give thanks: for this is the will of God in Christ Jesus concerning you" (1 Thessalonians 5:18). Develop a sincere attitude of gratitude and model it for your family and friends. Be thankful for all things great and small and let God know that you are (Philippians 4:6). Take time to give thanks before meals. Make it a point to say thank you to others

and mean it. Fill your speech with sincere expressions of thankfulness to God and man.

4. *Encourage others as they strive to be faithful.* Make it a practice to associate with members of the Lord's church at times and places other than worship. People of like interests and beliefs enjoy spending their leisure time together. Ephesians 4:12 tells us to "edify [build up, encourage] the body of Christ [fellow Christians]." A kind word spoken at the right time can make a huge difference in another Christian's life. Take every opportunity to give sincere encouragement to others. Worship regularly. Your presence is an encouragement to others as they seek to honor God and build their faith.

5. *Talk the talk and mean it!* Fill your conversations with sincere references to God's Son and His Word. The psalmist states, "Let the words of my mouth, and the meditation of my heart, be acceptable in thy sight, O Lord, my strength, and my redeemer" (Psalm 19:14).

 Although it may sound a bit trite, do ask yourself, "What would Jesus do, and what would Jesus say?" Your status as a follower of Christ should not be a mystery to your daily associates. Be a good example in word and deed without beating others over the head with your "goodness." They will know you belong to Christ if you are consistent and sincere in your efforts to do and say the right thing in every circumstance. Be careful to use a kind tone when you speak! Misplaced sarcasm or thoughtless comments may negatively affect the way others see you. If you are a caring person on the inside, make sure your "outside" shows it.

6. *Pray often.* One of the very best ways to strengthen your faith in God is to talk to Him daily. The Bible even gives

examples of whom to pray for and what to pray about. We can pray for ourselves as Jesus did (Hebrews 5:7). Pray for each other (James 5:16) and for our enemies (Luke 6:28; Matthew 5:44). We are told to pray for the ministers of the gospel (2 Thessalonians 3:1–2). Pray for the sick, which includes the spiritually sick (James 5:14–16). Remember the rulers of our country in prayer (1 Timothy 2:1–2), along with all men everywhere (1 Timothy 2:1). And pray always and without ceasing (Ephesians 6:18; 1 Thessalonians 5:17). Finally, we should ask God daily to increase our faith and make it stronger (Mark 9:24; Luke 17:5).

7. *Be proactive.* Create situations that are likely to bring forth good things rather than staying on guard to minimize the unavoidable messes of haphazard planning. How can women use their faith in God every day to protect and enrich lives? Review the previous steps and you will conclude that each step is proactive. The assurance that God loves us and gave His Son for us (John 3:16) is the fuel that enables us to plan and work fearlessly for His kingdom (2 Timothy 1:7). Let's be on the lookout for opportunities to study the Bible with friends and neighbors, to pray for them, and to speak kindly to them. We must be ready always to serve others, because our actions loudly proclaim our beliefs and convictions.

Adverse Side Effects of Faithfulness

Your physician may caution you to be watchful for negative side effects when you begin taking a new prescription. Similarly, Christians should expect to experience some adverse reactions as they demonstrate their continued faithfulness to God. Here are some common negative side effects of increased faithfulness.

🙰 *Doubt*—Doubt may creep into your thinking when you are feeling the most alone or weak. Friends may react to you differently once you become a faithful Christian. Family members may be doubtful of your sincerity. Others may ridicule your faith in God whom they cannot see. Recognize doubt and cast it out by giving aid to someone who needs help.

🙰 *Disobedience*—Disobedience is a silent condition that may slip into your thoughts and actions when you least expect it. It may come from within or from the comments and actions of others. What can encourage you to stumble in your Christian walk? Why will you disobey God? The most common reasons are the TV programs you watch, the books and magazines you read, and the friends you choose.

🙰 *Worry*—Worry is a feeling of uneasiness, apprehension, or dread. People who worry live in the future, spending a great deal of the present's time speculating on what might happen. They continually fear the worst. Anxiety, or a general feeling of uneasiness, often accompanies worry. Worry can steal years of a woman's time that could be used laboring in God's kingdom. Are you a worrier? Remind yourself that God is in charge at all times (Psalm 103:19). He knows everything (Job 7:20). And He is everywhere (Psalm 139:7).

At the first sign of an adverse side effect read:

1 Peter 5:7	John 14:27	Psalm 40:1–3
Isaiah 40:31	John 14:1–3	Isaiah 41:10
Psalm 32:7–9	Romans 8:31–32	John 14:18
Proverbs 3:5–6	James 1:2–4	Romans 8:24–25

WOMEN OF FAITH

Mary of Nazareth

Mary was a humble village maiden who lived in a town so insignificant that it led Nathaniel to say, "Can there any good thing come out of Nazareth?" (John 1:46.) As the mother of Jesus, Mary is better known than any female character in the Bible. She has long been the best-known woman in the world. The Bible does not tell us anything about her appearance or her family's importance. She was probably a poor teenager when she was espoused to Joseph.

- *Mary had a beautiful character.* Gabriel, the angel of the Lord, told her, "Blessed art thou among women" (Luke 1:28). However, just because she was called blessed doesn't mean that we should make her the object of our worship.

- *Mary was spiritually fit to be the mother of Jesus.* Following Gabriel's complimentary proclamation that she was highly favored, the angel of the Lord said, "The Lord is with thee" (Luke 1:28). Mary was obedient to God's will and was physically pure, as shown in the miracle of the virgin birth. She also was thankful to God and was humbled by His confidence in her (Luke 1:46–56).

- *Mary was human.* She needed a savior just as we do. Mary was not the mother of God as some teach; she was simply God's vessel to bring His Son to earth in human form. "But Mary kept all these things, and pondered them in her heart" (Luke 2:19). Mary's good attitude during that time probably influenced the rest of her life.

- *Mary was obedient.* Think about all the questions that must have run through her mind after Gabriel's visit! How did

God want her to raise His Son? Why was she chosen? How should she tell Joseph? These thoughts and so many more must have bombarded her, but she managed all of them well because she had faith in God and a willingness to do His will. "And Mary said, Behold the handmaid of the Lord; be it unto me according to thy word. And the angel departed from her" (Luke 1:38).

So far as we know, after Gabriel told Mary she would bear God's Son, she was never again visited by an angel. Joseph, not Mary, was told in a dream to go to Egypt in order to save the Christ child. As we read about Mary later in her life, we see her close to her Son, working continually to do His will (Mark 3:31–35; Acts 1:12–14).

God chose Mary to be the mother of Jesus because He knew she was able to hold fast to her faith, "the substance of things hoped for, the evidence of things not seen." She did not know the future, but she was compelled to accept, with the help of her faith, the astonishing announcements and the revealing challenges of being the mother of our Lord. Through joys and trials, she trusted her Son and she trusted her God. Don't you want to have a faith like Mary's?

Hannah

Hannah was the favorite wife of Elkanah. Sadly, she had no children. However, her husband's second wife, Peninnah, had several, and she delighted in taunting Hannah about her barrenness. Although her husband frequently reassured her of his love, Hannah's greatest desire was to be a mother.

After many years of barrenness, Hannah came to the tabernacle in Shiloh, where Eli was high priest, and prayed,

> O Lord of hosts, if thou wilt indeed look on the affliction of thine handmaid, and remember me, and not forget thine handmaid, but wilt give unto thine handmaid a man child,

then I will give him unto the Lord all the days of his life, and there shall no razor come upon his head (1 Samuel 1:11).

Note Hannah's attributes.

- *Hannah was selective.* Did Hannah run to her next door neighbor and bare her soul? Did she go to a fortune teller to see what the future might hold? No, she went to God for a prescription that would grant her heart's desire—a man-child.

- *Hannah was honest.* Eli questioned Hannah's actions and was able to understand her reasons for praying even though God had taken away her voice. He told her that God would answer her prayer. A few months later, Hannah's son, Samuel, was born. She loved him with all her heart and she remembered her promise to God. When he was old enough, Hannah took Samuel to Shiloh to live with Eli in the house of the Lord. Hannah was faithful to her promises to God; she honored her commitment.

- *Hannah was a servant.* Each year she visited her son and presented him a coat that she had made.

Hannah is an example of faith in action. Her honest, serving attitude was evidence of her trust in God. She put her hand in His hand and never looked back. Don't you want to have a faith like Hannah's?

QUESTIONS ABOUT YOUR PRESCRIPTION

1. Peter did not always have all the faith he needed. Why do you think that Peter worked diligently throughout his life to become a better Christian and to have stronger faith?

2. Discuss practical examples of a proactive faith.

3. Give three reasons why worry is counterproductive to the development and maintenance of faith.

4. Discuss some ways women today can attain the kind of faith Peter describes.

5. When Mary learned she was pregnant, what are some of the issues she had to be concerned with that involved her betrothed, Joseph? How did her faith help her in her approach?

6. How did Mary once express her faith in her own Son? (John 2:5.)

7. How do Mary's words in Luke 1:38 apply to us today?

8. Who remained at the cross after all the men had gone away? (John 19:25.)

9. What was Hannah's reaction when Eli told her that her prayer would be granted? Why do you think she believed him?

10. Hannah gave Samuel over to Eli for a life of service to God. How is that a good example of Hannah's faith?

11. Had you been in Hannah's place, how would you have felt about:

    a. being barren?

    b. snide remarks from Peninnah?

    c. Eli's accusation of your being drunk?

    d. God's promise of a son?

    e. turning your little boy over to a strange man to be mentored by him?

12. After discussing the above, give a summary of your perception of Hannah's faith.

FURTHER RESEARCH

∞ What did Rahab do to merit being listed in the "roll call of the faithful" in Hebrews 11?

∞ What statement did the woman with the issue of blood make that proved her faith?

∞ How can we tell the difference between our faith and our emotions?

CHAPTER 2

Virtue
THE SOUL'S COMPASS

PRESCRIPTION

And beside this, giving all diligence, add to your faith virtue; *and to virtue knowledge; and to knowledge temperance; and to temperance patience; and to patience godliness; and to godliness brotherly kindness; and to brotherly kindness charity* (2 Peter 1:5–7).

PHYSICIAN'S INSTRUCTIONS

Finally, brethren, whatsoever things are true, whatsoever things are honest, whatsoever things are just, whatsoever things are pure, whatsoever things are lovely, whatsoever things are of good report; if there be any virtue, and if there be any praise, think on these things (Philippians 4:8).

DAILY DOSE

2 Timothy 3:16–17   2 Timothy 2:22
Ephesians 5:15–16   Ruth 3:11
Proverbs 31:10–31

What Is Virtue?

As we continue our study of Peter's prescriptions for our souls, we find his next instruction to add virtue to our foundation of faith. Virtue is "moral excellence; goodness; righteousness; the quality of doing what is right and avoiding what is wrong; the ability to distinguish right from wrong and to choose what is right; right action and thinking; goodness of character."

These meanings all help us to understand virtue. However, there is only one true reference that defines virtue for us—God's Word. Cultivating virtue requires us to conform to God's standards of behavior and to live as He commands. The apostle Paul wrote:

> All scripture is given by inspiration of God, and is profitable for doctrine, for reproof, for correction, for instruction in righteousness: that the man [or woman] of God may be perfect, thoroughly furnished unto all good works (2 Timothy 3:16–17).

Our instructions in righteousness (virtue) must come from the Bible.

The Bible identifies some of the immoral practices that God explicitly condemns. Listen to this warning:

> Know ye not that the unrighteous shall not inherit the kingdom of God? Be not deceived: neither fornicators, nor idolaters, nor adulterers, nor effeminate, nor abusers of themselves with mankind, nor thieves, nor covetous, nor drunkards, nor revilers, nor extortioners, shall inherit the kingdom of God (1 Corinthians 6:9–10).

If God condemns people who engage in these kinds of sinful behaviors, it follows that a woman who wishes to nurture virtue in her life should refrain from any activity or thought connected with these practices. Many times, the key to deciding what something is begins with deciding what it is not. Thus, being virtuous is the exact opposite of being immoral.

Of course, virtue is much more than just avoiding what is bad. Virtue has vibrant moral power. A virtuous person possesses inner goodness and a desire to study God's Word. The psalmist sings, "O how I love thy law! It is my meditation all the day" (Psalm 119:97). Studying God's Word and meditating on its meaning are excellent ways to become more virtuous.

The need to add virtue to our faith is an easily understood concept. But how can we accomplish that? None of us will wake up tomorrow morning and find ourselves anointed with a new supply of virtue! We must be diligent in our study and prepared to do a great deal of work.

Virtue, the Soul's Compass: How Can I Develop It?

1. *Seek to be virtuous.* Anything worth having is worth working for. That is surely true about adding virtue to our faith. Making the conscious decision to be morally good—virtuous!—is the first step. We must always look to the Bible as our guidebook. Paul told Timothy: "Flee also youthful lusts: but follow righteousness, faith, charity, peace, with them that call on the Lord out of a pure heart" (2 Timothy 2:22). We, too, should actively work to add virtue to our personal character.

   Developing new skills is a gradual process. You didn't learn how to read or write overnight, and you can't build a virtuous character overnight. No one can make you desire virtue. When you seek to be virtuous, each good deed you do, each morally correct relationship you have, and each Bible chapter you read will add to your character's complexion. Before long, other people will be able to see the goodness within you by the way you treat others and yourself.

The most outstanding examples of virtue are God the Father and His Son Jesus. They always act in a virtuous manner and do what is righteous and good. We can gain virtue by becoming "imitators [followers] of God" (Ephesians 5:1). Peter tells us: "For even hereunto were ye called: because Christ also suffered for us, leaving us an example, that ye should follow his steps" (1 Peter 2:21).

2. *Eliminate anything in your life that is not morally excellent.* Examine your life and "clean house." Eliminate questionable friends, clothing, and activities. And remember, self-examination is not easy. Begin with courage. Am I kind? Am I honest? Am I a servant? What am I seeking first? Am I modest? Am I content?

God knew that women would need every ounce of their faith to work on becoming more Christ-like. Read the Bible, talk with Christian friends whom you trust, and perform acts of random kindness. So strive to be a better person today than you were yesterday. Every forward step will bring you closer to maturity as a Christian. Just be sure to keep in mind that following Peter's prescription involves continuous, positive change and forward movement.

3. *Take time from other activities to pursue virtue.* Our soul's compass is developed by reading and meditating on God's Word and then practicing what we learn. How does a woman learn to sew, cook, type, or drive? She makes a choice of how to invest the minutes and hours of every day. Paul directs us to "see then that ye walk circumspectly, not as fools, but as wise, redeeming the time, because the days are evil" (Ephesians 5:15–16). Virtue is developed just like every other trait: Practice, practice, practice.

The apostle Paul encouraged us specifically in the "Physician's Instructions": "If there be any virtue . . . think on these things." Why not make a list of things to think on and things to avoid? We must corral our thoughts, because thoughts are the springboard of all actions. What is the reward for pure thinking? Read this chapter's "Physician's Instructions" again: an entrance into Christ's eternal kingdom is promised.

Paul also tells us we can "come in the unity of the faith, and of the knowledge of the Son of God, unto a perfect man [or woman], unto the measure of the stature of the fulness of Christ" (Ephesians 4:13). And to encourage us, he says, "I press toward the mark for the prize of the high call-

MAKE A LIST OF THINGS TO THINK ON AND THINGS TO AVOID.

ing of God in Christ Jesus" (Philippians 3:14). Even Paul was in the process of becoming more virtuous each day. Make sure your daily thoughts and actions are better today than they were yesterday, the goal being to become complete (mature) in the Lord.

4. *Show modesty in all areas of your life.* Paul tells Timothy: "In like manner also, that women adorn themselves in modest apparel, with shamefacedness and sobriety" (1 Timothy 2:9). Why should Christian women dress in clothes that show the seriousness of their commitment to living a Christian life? Often we hear a woman say, "Well, what if this blouse shows a little cleavage? What's wrong with that?" Reverse that thought and ask, "What is right with it?" Of course, this doesn't mean a Christian woman's wardrobe must be black and filled with skirts that brush the floor, but neither does it mean she can have clothes that are revealing and sexually stimulating. Clothe yourself, not to reveal your physical body, but to reveal your

"meek and quiet spirit." Allow others to see Christ living in you (Colossians 1:27; John 15:4).

Modesty also includes the way we interact with other people. A modest woman won't try to be the center of attention in every situation, nor will she brag on herself and her accomplishments. Paul says Christians should "live sensibly, righteously and godly in the present age" (Titus 2:12). Surely, modesty is a part of living righteously and godly!

Adverse Side Effects of Becoming More Virtuous

As you become more virtuous each day, you can expect that Satan will seek to undermine your efforts in any way possible. Paul was well aware of this fact when he told the church at Ephesus:

> Put on the whole armor of God that ye may be able to stand against the wiles of the devil. For we wrestle not against flesh and blood, but against principalities, against powers, against the rulers of the darkness of this world, against spiritual wickedness in high places. Wherefore take unto you the whole armor of God that ye may be able to withstand in the evil day, and having done all, to stand (Ephesians 6:11–13).

Some of the negative side effects of becoming more virtuous may be:

∞ *Selfishness*—Sometimes a person is so focused on becoming more virtuous or righteous that she begins to exclude other aspects of her Christian life and even the needs of other Christians (1 Corinthians 10:24). Paul told the members of the church at Philippi,

> Let nothing be done through strife or vainglory; but in lowliness of mind let each esteem other better than

themselves. Look not every man on his own things, but every man also on the things of others (Philippians 2:3–4).

Selfishness such as this described by Paul can creep into our lives even as we work diligently to become stronger and better Christians.

> *Prevention:* Be alert and watchful of your intentions and actions. Our goal must be to stay focused on the needs of others more than our own. Paul instructed Timothy, "Be rich in good works, ready to distribute, willing to communicate" (1 Timothy 6:18). A growing, healthy Christian is always on the lookout for the first symptoms of selfishness.

℀ *Fear*—As you strive to mature in Christ, fear might creep into your innermost thoughts. Fear is an unwelcome by-product of self-examination and the struggle to remove anything that might tarnish your virtuous character. Fear of being tainted by the sinful aspects of the world can paralyze growing Christians. Paul refers to this condition in 2 Timothy 1:7, "For God hath not given us the spirit of fear; but of power, and of love, and of a sound mind," and we can see that it is not from God.

> *Prevention:* If you know that the fear of worldly evils has begun to grow in your mind, go to the Bible for strength and assurance. Paul tells the Christians at Philippi,
>
>> Be careful for nothing; but in every thing by prayer and supplication with thanksgiving let your requests be made known unto God. And the peace of God, which passeth all understanding, shall keep your hearts and minds through Christ Jesus (Philippians 4:6–7).

Peter instructs his readers:

> Humble yourselves therefore under the mighty hand of God, that he may exalt you in due time: casting all your care upon him; for he careth for you (1 Peter 5:6–7).

∞ *Self-righteousness*—Some Christian women and girls have allowed their godly self-assurance to become tainted gradually by self-righteousness. This means they have become convinced of their own righteousness and are completely intolerant of the opinions and behavior of others. Caution! Do not to fall into this way of thinking.

> *Prevention:* The Bible is our only standard for matters of doctrine. However, matters of opinion may vary among Christians. To guard against a self-righteous attitude, remember the Roman Christians. They had "a zeal of God, but not according to knowledge," and "being ignorant of God's righteousness, and going about to establish their own righteousness, have not submitted themselves unto the righteousness of God" (Romans 10:2–3). Yes, righteousness is of God and self-righteousness is condemned,
>
> > And be found in him [Christ], not having mine own righteousness, which is of the law, but that which is through the faith of Christ, the righteousness which is of God by faith (Philippians 3:9).

Women of Virtue

Ruth

What a virtuous woman! Ruth's story unfolds in the Old Testament book that bears her name. She is one of only two women for whom a book of the Bible was named. Boaz told her: "And now, my daughter, fear not; I will do to thee all that thou requirest: for all the city of my people doth know that thou art a virtuous woman" (Ruth 3:11).

Ruth is an example of the rewards of loyalty and moral goodness. She was a young woman in Moab—present-day Jordan—who married Mahlon, one of the sons of Elimelech and Naomi. Elimelech's family had fled Israel during the time of the judges because of a severe famine. They began a new life in Moab. Their other son Chilion married a Moabitess named Orpah.

RUTH'S STATEMENT OF LOYALTY AND LOVE REFLECTED HER SOUL'S VIRTUE.

After a few years, Elimelech and both his sons died leaving Naomi alone with her two daughters-in-law. Of course, Naomi's thoughts turned to the security of her own home and family back in the land of Judah, so she prepared to return to Bethlehem. When she blessed her daughters-in-law and bade them farewell, Orpah kissed her and departed for her own mother's house. Ruth had greater things in mind, and she freely expressed her decision to Naomi.

> Intreat me not to leave thee, or to return from following after thee: for whither thou goest, I will go; and where thou lodgest, I will lodge: thy people shall be my people, and thy God my God: Where thou diest, will I die, and there will I be buried: the Lord do so to me, and more also, if ought but death part thee and me (Ruth 1:16–17).

Ruth's statement of loyalty and love is a clear reflection of the goodness and virtue that lived in her soul.

Naomi returned with Ruth to Bethlehem. Ruth comforted her mother-in-law and looked for ways to support her. Naomi suggested that she go into the fields of Boaz, her husband's kinsman, and gather the wheat that the reapers dropped. Ruth did as she was told, all the while conducting herself in a chaste and virtuous manner. Boaz immediately noticed the young woman and asked about her identity. When he learned she was the widow of one of his kinsmen, he told her to stay in his fields so she would be safe. Ruth obeyed and continued to gather wheat there.

Ruth told Naomi of Boaz's actions. Naomi knew Boaz was capable of providing safety and comfort for both her and Ruth for the rest of their lives. Therefore, she told Ruth to dress in her best clothes and to go to the threshing floor where she expected Boaz to sleep that night. Naomi instructed her to wait until he slept and then uncover his feet and lie down. Naomi's instructions were in accordance with Moses' law:

> If brethren dwell together, and one of them die, and have no child, the wife of the dead shall not marry without unto a stranger: her husband's brother shall go in unto her, and take her to him to wife, and perform the duty of an husband's brother unto her (Deuteronomy 25:5).

Boaz was a close kinsman of Naomi's deceased husband. That kinship satisfied God's directive.

When Boaz realized that Ruth was lying near him, he assured her that he knew she was a virtuous woman and that he would fulfill his obligations to her. He first had to make sure that another kinsman didn't wish to marry her. After doing this, Boaz married Ruth and cared for her and Naomi until death.

If Ruth had been a forward or aggressive woman, this story would have ended very differently. Her loyalty and obedience to Naomi, coupled with her chaste behavior, communicated the kind of person she was to everyone who knew her. Ruth's character and actions are truly examples to young women today whose "idols" may be promiscuous and lazy.

The Woman in Proverbs 31

Proverbs 31:10 asks, "Who can find a virtuous woman? For her worth is far above rubies." The life and actions of the woman in Proverbs 31 define her as courageous, strong, pure, and godly. She is an excellent example for us to study. That fact is further affirmed in verse 10: "Her price is far above rubies."

A virtuous woman:

—is trustworthy (v. 11)
—is supportive of her husband and his activities (vv. 12, 23)
—is an industrious and hard worker (v. 13)
—cares for her family with food (vv. 14–15)
—is intelligent, capable of making business decisions (v. 16)
—takes care of her physical health (v. 17)
—is watchful, plans for the future (v. 18)
—is able to take care of herself and others, especially the needy (vv. 19–20)
—is not upset by unforeseen circumstances because she has made preparations for problems (vv. 21–22)
—is supportive of her husband's activities (v. 23)
—makes and sells handiwork (v. 24)
—is prepared, strong, and honorable (v. 25)
—is kind and wise when she speaks (v. 26)
—works instead of "eating the bread of idleness" (v. 27)
—is praised by her husband and children and is called "blessed" (v. 28)
—seeks the Lord's gifts instead of favor and beauty (v. 30)
—achieves her desires, with the Lord's help (v. 31)

What better recipe for virtue can we find? Of course, the answer is "none." These qualities, along with Peter's prescription to add virtue to our faith, emphasize to all Christian women the importance of being virtuous—acting and thinking in a morally good manner.

QUESTIONS ABOUT YOUR PRESCRIPTION

1. Discuss some of the consequences of behaving immodestly.

2. Ruth's words to Naomi in Ruth 1:16–17 are some of the most beautiful in the Bible. How do you account for her determination to go with Naomi, especially in light of the fact that she did not descend from Israel?

3. Why do you think Boaz noticed Ruth gathering after the reapers? Were his intentions honorable or dishonorable? Why?

4. When Naomi sent Ruth to the threshing floor to lie at the feet of Boaz, what were her intentions? Were her actions honorable or dishonorable?

5. It has been said that Ruth was the first woman mentioned in the Bible who proposed to her husband. Did she? What gave her that right?

6. Find evidence in both the Old Testament and the New Testament that Ruth was David's great-grandmother.

7. Explain what "strength and honor are her clothing" means in Proverbs 31:25.

8. What is another way of saying, "She eateth not the bread of idleness"? (Proverbs 31:27.)

9. If your children do not "rise up and call you blessed," does that mean you are not a virtuous woman? Why or why not?

10. How may a single woman be considered virtuous by God and man?

11. Which of the virtuous woman's traits would you choose for your own daughter?

FURTHER RESEARCH

☙ Can Queen Vashti (Esther 1:11) be thought of as an example of virtue? What did she do and why?

☙ Mary, the mother of Jesus, was certainly a woman of virtue. What concern did she express to the angel of the Lord about her condition in Luke 2:24?

☙ What was the circumstance when Jesus felt virtue flow out of Him? Comment on that event.

CHAPTER 3

Knowledge
THE KEY

PRESCRIPTION

And beside this, giving all diligence, add to your faith virtue; and to virtue knowledge; *and to knowledge temperance; and to temperance patience; and to patience godliness; and to godliness brotherly kindness; and to brotherly kindness charity* (2 Peter 1:5–7).

PHYSICIAN'S INSTRUCTIONS

[The Bereans] were more fair-minded than those in Thessalonica, in that they received the word with all readiness, and searched the Scriptures daily to find out whether these things were so (Acts 17:11 NKJV).

DAILY DOSE

Ephesians 5:17	2 Timothy 3:6–7
Romans 15:4	2 Timothy 2:15
1 Timothy 2:4	

What Is Knowledge?

Knowledge is "an understanding of facts, truths, or principles, as from study or investigation." Let's examine Peter's "soul prescription" as he directs us to add to our faith and virtue an understanding of the facts, truths, and principles of God's Word.

WOULD YOU PLAY A GAME WITHOUT RULES?

The kind of knowledge Peter prescribed for first century Christians is more than general intelligence or an understanding about the world. His message is this: Strive to gain knowledge about Christ and His church. What is the benefit of a deeper and more complete knowledge? It equips us to withstand temptations and assaults on our faith that are sure to come.

Keep in mind that Peter was inspired by God through the Holy Spirit. He knew and understood the deeper things of God, Christ, and the church. Through inspiration he gave us the prescription for knowledge. He understood the continuing need for the assurance and encouragement that only knowledge of the Lord and His church can bring.

Know the Rules

Gaining knowledge of God's Word enables us to understand more easily the difference between acceptable and unacceptable behavior for Christians. Would you volunteer to play a game without first understanding the rules and knowing what is required of you? The Christian life is much more than a game, yet many who call themselves Christians have no idea how to behave. Just saying "I am a Christian" doesn't make you one, anymore than saying you are a singer or an engineer makes you one. To be seen as a true Christian, singer, or engineer, we must remember that having the proper knowledge is of utmost importance.

Peter doesn't tell us to increase our knowledge just for the sake of getting smarter. He tells us to increase our understanding so we can grow into God-centered, loving, productive people. That's why we should want to know all we can about God's Word, His Son, and the church.

How Much and What Kind?

How much knowledge do we need? What kind of knowledge should we pursue? Hosea 4:6 states, "My people are destroyed for lack of knowledge." We may conclude that we can have too little knowledge! A lack of knowledge is fatal. Just as we must eat our daily bread, we must also seek daily biblical knowledge. Regular Bible study assures us of a continual supply of spiritual knowledge.

Ephesians 5:17 directs, "Wherefore be ye not unwise, but understanding what the will of the Lord is." Proverbs 23:23 says, "Buy the truth, and sell it not; also wisdom, and instruction, and understanding." David wrote in Psalm 119:66, "Teach me good judgment and knowledge: for I have believed thy commandments." A wise woman seeks the kind of knowledge that enables her to understand the will of God. This includes good judgment, instruction, and understanding. Wisdom is the sum of knowledge and experience.

MY PEOPLE ARE DESTROYED FOR LACK OF KNOWLEDGE.
—HOSEA 4:6

The Bible also talks about the kinds of knowledge to avoid. Remember what God told Adam and Eve: "But of the tree of the knowledge of good and evil, thou shalt not eat of it: for in the day that thou eatest thereof thou shalt surely die" (Genesis 2:17). Paul described to Timothy the kind of people who think they are wise, but are not:

For of this sort are they which creep into houses, and lead captive silly women laden with sins, led away with divers lusts, ever learning, and never able to come to the knowledge of the truth (2 Timothy 3:6–7).

When you are studying a subject ask yourself: "Does this lead me to knowledge of the truth?" One lady remarked, "Some things I don't need to know!" Knowledge about worldly and sinful things is certainly not the kind of knowledge Peter prescribed!

Knowledge the Key—How Can I Develop It?

൦ഌ *Study and practice.* How do you acquire knowledge on any subject? Proverbs 1:5 tells us, "A wise man [woman] will hear, and will increase learning; and a man of understanding shall attain unto wise counsels." Paul states in his letter to the church in Rome, "For whatsoever things were written aforetime were written for our learning, that we through patience and comfort of the scriptures might have hope" (Romans 15:4). He also encouraged the young preacher Timothy to study to show himself "approved unto God, a workman that needeth not to be ashamed, rightly dividing the word of truth" (2 Timothy 2:15).

൦ഌ *Desire salvation.* Perhaps the most compelling reason to pursue knowledge is because God wants everyone "to be saved and to come unto the knowledge of the truth" (1 Timothy 2:4). We should desire to gain knowledge of the truth because it is God's will! Paul restates his desire for all to have knowledge of God:

> That ye [everyone, everywhere] might walk worthy of the Lord unto all pleasing, being fruitful in every

good work, and increasing in the knowledge of God (Colossians 1:10).

And finally, our own "Dr. Peter" gives these directions: "But grow in grace, and in the knowledge of our Lord and Savior Jesus Christ. To him be glory both now and for ever. Amen" (2 Peter 3:18).

What is more important than our knowing the truth? John tells us, "Sanctify them through thy truth: thy word is truth" (John 17:17). If the truth is God's Word, then God's people, the church, have these obligations:

—*The church must know the truth.* "And ye shall know the truth, and the truth shall make you free" (John 8:32).

—*The church must uphold the truth.* "But if I tarry long, that thou mayest know how thou oughtest to behave thyself in the house of God, which is the church of the living God, the pillar and ground of the truth" (1 Timothy 3:15).

—*The church must teach the truth.* "But speaking the truth in love, may grow up into him in all things, which is the head, even Christ" (Ephesians 4:14).

—*The church must defend the truth.* "But the other of love, knowing that I am set for the defense of the gospel" (Philippians 1:17).

Adverse Side Effects of Becoming More Knowledgeable

≈ *Pride*—"Pride brings destruction and a haughty spirit before a fall. It is better to be of a humble spirit with the lowly than to live it up among the rich and famous" (Proverbs 16:18–19). Throughout Scripture we are continually told about the negative consequences of pride. Satan was cast out of heaven because of pride (Isaiah 14:12–15). James

4:6 tells us God resists the proud but gives grace to the humble

Why is pride so sinful?

1. Pride gives self the credit for something that God has accomplished.

2. Pride takes the glory that belongs to God alone and claims it for self.

3. Pride is essentially self-worship. Anything we accomplish in this world is not possible unless God enables and sustains us.

That is why we give God the glory . . . for He alone deserves it. (James 4:6).

ෙ *Self-Importance*—A very real pitfall of becoming knowledgeable is the development of a feeling of self-importance. That attitude can appear gradually and without any warning signs. We have all met "experts" who make us feel as if their opinions are the only correct ones. To counter these kinds of people, Paul remind us: "For by grace are ye saved through faith; and that not of yourselves: it is the gift of God: not of works, lest any man should boast" (Ephesians 2:8–9). Needless to say, this statement pretty well puts the "experts" of the world in their places.

ෙ *Arrogance*—Arrogance is a very close cousin to self-importance and an equally dangerous side effect to gaining knowledge. An arrogant person differs slightly from a self-important one by the way she views herself. Self-important people know a great deal and want to be the first ones to share their knowledge, while arrogant people give the impression that they are naturally smarter than others. How dare anyone attempt to be as smart as they!

Samuel deals with arrogant people this way, "Talk no more so exceeding proudly; let not arrogance come out of your mouth; for the Lord is a God of knowledge, and by Him actions are weighed" (1 Samuel 2:3). Solomon adds, "The fear of the Lord is to hate evil; pride and arrogance and the evil way and the froward mouth do I hate" (Proverbs 8:13). And lest there be any doubt about how God views arrogance, note these words:

> And I will punish the world for their evil and the wicked for their iniquity; and I will cause the arrogance of the proud to cease, and will lay low the haughtiness of the terrible (Isaiah 13:11).

WOMEN OF KNOWLEDGE

Priscilla

Priscilla, along with her husband Aquila, is mentioned several times in the New Testament (Acts 18:2, 26; Romans 16:3; 1 Corinthians 16:19; 2 Timothy 4:19). This converted Jewish couple worked as tentmakers. With each mention of Priscilla, a mention is also made of Aquila. That leads us to believe they did almost everything together, including their daily work and teaching others about Christ.

THEY TOOK APOLLOS ASIDE AND EXPLAINED TO HIM THE WAY OF GOD MORE ACCURATELY.

Priscilla and Aquila had been expelled from Rome and had traveled to Corinth to live. Corinth was then the major government and trade center of the region. A superb seaport served as a crossroads for trade and travel. At least twelve temples there were dedicated to various gods and goddesses, including the notorious temple of Aphrodite whose followers practiced religious prostitution. At least a thousand prostitutes lounged on the temple steps. Obviously, a person could find almost any kind of sinful activity imaginable on the streets of Corinth.

Mighty Apollos

When Paul came to Corinth on his second missionary journey, he met Priscilla and Aquila. Since they shared common vocations (tent making) and religious convictions, Priscilla and Aquila asked Paul to live with them. Paul stayed with them for about eighteen months while preaching and teaching the gospel of Christ. Their relationship with Paul became so close that they moved with him to Ephesus when he continued his missionary journey.

> Now a certain Jew named Apollos, born at Alexandria, an eloquent man and mighty in the Scriptures, came to Ephesus. This man had been instructed in the way of the Lord; and being fervent in spirit, he spoke and taught accurately the things of the Lord, though he knew only the baptism of John (Acts 18:24–25).

Priscilla and Aquila heard Apollos when he spoke in the synagogue. Because he talked only about John's baptism, they recognized he did not have a complete knowledge of the gospel of Christ. They took him aside and taught him more fully about God's plan through His Son—Jesus' death, burial, and resurrection (Acts 18:26).

Now we come to the reason Priscilla was chosen as an example of our knowledge prescription. The Bible tells us that both Aquila and Priscilla explained to him the way of God more accurately. Priscilla knew the complete gospel of Christ and was able to teach Apollos what he should do to be saved.

From the Scriptures

Notice that Priscilla taught Apollos in a private meeting, not from the pulpit. This divine example makes it clear that women can teach men in private situations. The New Testament records no instance of a woman's preaching to a group of Christians. In fact, the practice of a woman's speaking during the worship of the church is condemned by Paul: "Let your women keep silent in the churches, for they are not permitted to speak; but they are to be submissive, as the law also says."

What were the results of Priscilla's and Aquila's teachings? Apollos became an excellent leader and guide to those who by grace had believed. "For he vigorously refuted [proved the error of] the Jews in public debate, proving from the Scriptures that Jesus was the Christ" (Acts 18:27–28). Priscilla's teaching serves as an excellent example to us that knowledgeable women can teach the Scriptures to anyone in a private situation.

Lois and Eunice

Lois and her daughter Eunice are mentioned only once in the Bible:

> Having been reminded of the unfeigned [sincere] faith that is in you; which lived first in your grandmother Lois, and your mother Eunice, and, I am persuaded, in you also (1 Timothy 1:5).

These women in Timothy's life probably did not have many material things; most women in those days had little of this world's goods. They had to work very hard since they had no timesaving devices such as automatic washing machines or even indoor water faucets and bathrooms. Their days were most likely consumed with getting and preparing food for Timothy, his Greek father, and themselves.

However, Lois and Eunice obviously made time to ensure that the young Timothy learned about Jesus and His plan of salvation. Just imagine the energy they used and the determination they must have had! Thanks be to God that Eunice and Lois knew Christ and that they made sure that Timothy did, also.

What was the fruit of their knowledge of Christ and their love and devotion to Timothy? He grew up to be a gospel preacher, a fellow missionary of Paul, and a morally good person. Because of the knowledge and faith of his mother and grandmother, Timothy became a man of God who, more than two thousand years later, is still remembered and respected.

QUESTIONS ABOUT YOUR PRESCRIPTION

1. How can we acquire knowledge of God's will for us?

2. What is your favorite method of Bible study? Make a brief statement about your method of intense Bible study.

3. If you could have a face-to-face meeting with a popular female television evangelist, what would you say concerning her public preaching?

4. Discuss some of the positive characteristics of Priscilla and Aquila's relationship.

5. If someone asked you who Jesus is and how to become part of His church, how would you use the Bible to tell them? (Hint: Highlighting scripture references is great help for teachers. Not all of us can memorize lengthy scripture quotations—nor do we need to.)

6. What was the fruit of Priscilla and Aquila's teachings?

7. What did Lois and Eunice do to help mold Timothy's character?

8. What special relationship did the apostle Paul have with Timothy?

9. Why are Lois and Eunice good examples of the attribute of knowledge as discussed in 2 Peter 1:5–7?

10. If you know a "Lois and Timothy" relationship, share it with the class. What does your "Lois" do to keep the Lord in her "Timothy's" life?

FURTHER RESEARCH

∾ Can Mary and Martha be considered good examples of women who had knowledge about Jesus Christ and His church? Why or why not? (See Luke 10:38–42; John 11:1–45; John 12:1–7.)

∾ Discuss the knowledge mentioned in 1 Corinthians 8:10–11.

∾ How do you reconcile sinful pride and self-confidence?

CHAPTER 4

Temperance
THE BOUNDARY

PRESCRIPTION

And beside this, giving all diligence, add to your faith virtue; and to virtue knowledge; and to knowledge temperance; *and to temperance patience; and to patience godliness; and to godliness brotherly kindness; and to brotherly kindness charity* (2 Peter 1:5–7).

PHYSICIAN'S INSTRUCTIONS

But the fruit of the Spirit is love, joy, peace, longsuffering, gentleness, goodness, faith, meekness, temperance: against such there is no law. And they that are Christ's have crucified the flesh with the affections and lusts (Galatians 5:22–24).

DAILY DOSE

Romans 12:12   Proverbs 25:16
1 Corinthians 13:11   Daniel 1:8
2 Timothy 1:7

What Is Temperance?

Temperance is "having moderation or self-restraint in actions, statements; the avoidance of excesses in one's life." Other words that mean about the same as temperance are constraint, prudence, sobriety, and self-control. We are instructed by our "Prescription" to strengthen our faith, virtue, and knowledge with a liberal dose of temperance. We should strive to be Christian women who are not given to excesses in any area of our lives.

SELF-CONTROL HOLDS HANDS WITH CONTENTMENT.

In the United States, temperance is often associated with the anti-alcohol crusades of the early twentieth century. In fact, one of the major organizations whose members campaigned against the use of alcoholic drinks was called the Women's Christian Temperance Union. It's easy to see that the use of the word *temperance* in this respect meant drinking little or no alcohol, but the meaning of temperance is much broader than that.

I Have Enough

Peter wrote his prescription to give us resources for resisting the enticing powers of evil. He knew that everything that looks good, tastes good, feels good, smells good, and sounds good may not necessarily be good for us. Any worldly activity, person, occupation, academic endeavor, or other undertaking that has power over us and takes up the majority of our time and resources is not good for us. Self-control holds hands with contentment. Make it your motto to say, "I have enough."

Some Christian women are careful to practice temperance in their sexual activities and cravings, while others work to bridle their tongues or control their eating and drinking. All of us must practice temperance and self-control in our most vulnerable areas. Romans 12:1–2 instructs us to present ourselves to God, not conforming to the world. Doing anything to excess—beyond what is sufficient—is not Christ-like. In this day of microwave mentality, not only do we want a lot of everything, we want it now! Note the wisdom of this proverb: "Hast thou found honey? eat so much as is sufficient for thee, lest thou be filled therewith, and vomit it" (Proverbs 25:16). In other words, too much, even of good things, can bring about very negative and unappealing consequences.

Spirit Needs Food, Water, and Pruning

Our "Physician's Instructions" tells us,

> But the fruit of the Spirit is love, joy, peace, longsuffering, gentleness, goodness, faith, meekness, temperance: against such there is no law. And they that are Christ's have crucified the flesh with the affections and lusts (Galatians 5:22–24).

Paul calls these qualities "fruit of the Spirit." Which apple trees produce sweet, juicy apples? Those nurtured, pruned, watered, and generally well-tended! Likewise, a Christian who is well-tended and disciplined by God's Word will produce the kind of fruit Paul describes. Temperance gives us boundaries of balance. Without it we are sure to neglect our spiritual necessities.

Certainly, some Christians deal with situations much more crucial than whether or not to eat another bite of candy. The news media are filled with tragic stories of young women in need of temperance. Some of these women have uncontrolled appetites for drugs or alcohol, while others exhibit unrestrained sexual behaviors. Hearing about the consequences of gambling, gossip, and many other sins of the flesh drives home the desperate need we all have for souls blessed with temperance and self-control. We can be assured that Peter knew this when he wrote these prescriptions for our souls.

Temperance, the Boundary: How Can I Develop It?

∞ *Put away childish behavior.* Are we born with temperance? Children have very little "stopping sense" when it comes to something that gratifies their desires. Problems arise when adults continue to behave as children. Paul plainly told the Corinthian brethren, "When I was a child, I spake as a child, I understood as a child, I thought as a child: but when I became a man, I put away childish things" (1 Corinthians 13:11). Many Christians fail to follow his example. When we are pouting or discontented, it is time for self-examination. When a Christian woman insists on having her own way and refuses to adhere to God's way, she parades her immaturity and disgraces the church. She is still taking a spiritual bottle rather than solid food. One woman told me, "We certainly have a lot of fat babies in this church!" How sad. Let's take the following passage to heart and grow up!

> That we henceforth be no more children, tossed to and fro, and carried about with every wind of doctrine, by the sleight of men, and cunning craftiness, whereby they lie in wait to deceive; but speaking the truth in love, may grow up into him in all things, which is the head, even Christ (Ephesians 4:14–15).

∞ *Depend on God's help.* When we attempt to practice discipline, we have to depend on God's help. If we depend only on the "self" in self-control we will surely fail. Paul told Timothy that God gave us a spirit "of power and love and discipline" (2 Timothy 1:7 ASV). We should ask for support and guidance from God as we work to become more temperate people. If we try to do everything entirely by ourselves, disappointment will certainly be the result.

ဆ *Be submissive to God's will.* Gaining a temperate spirit is a strenuous process. At times you may struggle and fail, but true failure comes only if you give up completely. After all, the ultimate goal of all of this work is to make the will of God our own will. As Christians, we don't belong solely to ourselves; we've been bought with a price.

> What? know ye not that your body is the temple of the Holy Ghost which is in you, which ye have of God, and ye are not your own? For ye are bought with a price: therefore glorify God in your body, and in your spirit, which are God's (1 Corinthians 6:19–20).

> Let every soul be subject unto the higher powers. For there is no power but of God: the powers that be are ordained of God (Romans 13:1).

ဆ *Watch for signs of weakness or failure.* Even the apostle Paul had to do this: "But I keep under my body, and bring it into subjection: lest that by any means, when I have preached to others, I myself should be a castaway" (1 Corinthians 9:26–27). We can be sure Satan stands ready to attack our weakest point.

Our actions and thoughts should not control us; we must control them. Saying "I have self-control" and then proving it are two entirely different matters. A skeptic once said, "Christianity has not so much been tried and found wanting, as been found difficult and left untried." Expect to be tired and even discouraged at times, but don't remain tired and discouraged all the time. Through prayer, study, and practice, we can follow Peter's prescription and add temperance to our Christian natures.

Adverse Side Effects of Temperance

Stumbling in the pursuit of a temperate nature can happen easily. This may be due, in part, to the fact that the human spirit possesses the capacity for so many desires and needs. As you strive to become more temperate, you may need to watch for the following negative effects.

- *Jealousy*— Learning to be temperate in all things is difficult! Even after a Christian woman has identified her target areas and worked diligently to control her desires, jealousy can sneak up on her. A glimpse of someone else relishing just the thing that she cannot enjoy can bring a fit of envy to even the most disciplined woman. "Why can she have two desserts and never gain an ounce? Why does she always have extra money? Why does she have the glamorous career?" This dangerous side effect shouts, "Why her and not me!" Paul warns us in Galatians 5:26, "Let us not be desirous of vain glory, provoking one another, envying one another." This exhortation is not a suggestion; it is a command.

- *Anger*—How can anger be a negative consequence of striving to be more temperate? It is easy to pass blame to God or family members for our own situations! Irritation over the huge effort it takes to overcome an especially strong desire can easily turn into anger at ourselves, others, and even God. "It is not fair!" is the cry of many angry women. When you have this side effect, recall Ephesians 4:31: "Let all bitterness and wrath and anger and clamor and evil speaking be put away from you, with all malice." All five of these sins lead to hatred, and even murder. Paul instructs us to get rid of them!

- *Evil thoughts*—One evil thought can undo in an instant the self-control that took many hours to build. God made us the masters of our bodies and minds, and He expects us to strive to be in control. What should we think about? "Whatsoever things are true, whatsoever things are honest, whatsoever things are just, whatsoever things are pure, whatsoever things are lovely, whatsoever things are of good report" (Philippians 4:8). Filling our minds with righteous thoughts leaves less space for evil thoughts when they come. God will help us reach our goal of temperance if we take the time to ask Him. "Be careful for nothing; but in every thing by prayer and supplication with thanksgiving let your requests be made known unto God" (Philippians 4:6).

WOMEN OF TEMPERANCE

Vashti

Vashti was the wife of King Ahasuerus of Persia, whose empire stretched "from India even unto Ethiopia, over an hundred and seven and twenty provinces" (Esther 1:1). This area encompasses present-day Turkey, Syria, Jordan, Israel, Iraq, Iran, Afghanistan, and Pakistan. Obviously, her husband was a very rich and powerful ruler. Read about Vashti in Esther 1.

On the third anniversary of his reign, the king decided to host a great feast for his subordinate rulers. He invited all the neighboring "nobles and princes of the provinces, being before him" (Esther 1:3). Such celebrations were usually for the purpose of displaying the host's power and wealth. The Bible tells us Ahasuerus "showed the riches of his glorious kingdom and the honor of his excellent majesty" for 180 days! (Esther 1:4).

After six months of partying, the king made another feast for all the residents of the capital city of Shushan. It was held in the garden of the palace and lasted for seven days. The decorations were beautiful, multicolored hangings with silver rings and pillars of marble. There were beds of gold and silver resting on pavements of red, blue, white, and black marble. In short, it was a breathtaking spectacle.

The king served royal wine in golden glasses to everyone who wished to drink it. It is doubtful that many abstained from drinking at the king's table. It also stands to reason that by the seventh day, the king and all the other notable male guests were very much intoxicated.

Meanwhile, Queen Vashti entertained the female guests in her royal house. Everything was progressing well until the king—whose "heart was merry with wine"—issued a royal order to his chamberlain to bring Queen Vashti that she might "show the people and princes her beauty; for she was fair to look on" (Esther 1:11).

Keep in mind that all of this took place in an Eastern society which separated the sexes in public. The king was entertaining the men while Vashti was entertaining the women. Now, Ahasuerus, who was drunken with wine, ordered Vashti to parade herself in front of all the noblemen of the region. She was told to wear her crown. Some believe the king's order was for to wear only her crown! Whatever the case, Vashti refused the king's order outright.

She said "No!"

Imagine the horror and intrigue the people felt when they got word that the queen had flatly refused to do the bidding of their king. The Jewish historian Flavius Josephus states that Vashti was asked several times to appear and refused each time. If this is the case, think of the embarrassment King Ahasuerus must have felt. Not only had his wife refused to do what he asked, she had refused in the presence of hundreds of dignitaries.

This story is filled with examples of intemperate people who exercised no self-control. Partying for 180 days leaves little doubt about the prudence or temperance King Ahasuerus possessed. Then, reeling from the effects of his party mood, the king chose to show off his "trophy wife." It's fairly plain to see that his actions were sexually motivated, as were those of the men at the party.

Vashti has been called a disobedient wife, one who needed punishment for refusing to obey her husband. I certainly don't see her that way. She appears to be a woman whose values were higher than her husband's. She refused to parade herself in front of intoxicated and baseminded men. No doubt, her modesty was the reason for her refusal. Just picture in your mind what the scene might have been if she had obeyed her husband. Lascivious men would have been leering at her. She might have been forced to dance nude in their presence. And all of this would have taken place in the presence of the one person who should have protected her dignity and virtue at all costs—her husband.

IT IS OFTEN EASY TO FALL IN WITH THE CROWD, BUT WHAT DOES GOD WANT?

Vashti took a great risk when she refused to come to the king. He had complete and total power over all his subjects, including the queen. With one sentence he could take her life or save it. Yet Vashti had enough temperance and modesty to refuse him. Her personal values and morals were more important to her than the world's acceptance or even her life.

For all these reasons, Vashti is an excellent example of temperance for girls and women today. It is often easy to fall in with the will of the crowd, but a Christian woman should always measure her actions against the standard of temperance. What does God want? Peter knew that our souls would need to be fortified with temperance and self-control in order for us to live a Christ-like life. His prescription is certainly the correct one for us.

Jochebed

Jochebed deserved a mother-of-the-year award. She showed tremendous self-control at a time when her baby boy's life depended on it. In Numbers 26:59 we're told, "And the name of Amram's wife was Jochebed, the daughter of Levi, whom her mother bare to Levi in Egypt: and she bare unto Amram Aaron and Moses, and Miriam their sister."

Jochebed and Amram were among the Hebrews who lived in Egypt when a new king came to power—a pharaoh who did not remember the goodness of Joseph. Fearing that Joseph's people would multiply and overthrow his government, Pharaoh put them into slavery and made them perform back-breaking labor. They continued to multiply, even in the face of his bitter treatment. Finally, in an attempt to decrease their population, he ordered the Hebrew midwives to cast all boy babies born to Hebrew mothers into the river Nile. When they didn't obey him, Pharaoh commanded the Egyptians to make sure all male Hebrew babies died in the river.

WHY DID SHE HIDE HER SON? SHE BELIEVED HE WAS SPECIAL TO GOD.

Jochebed was pregnant at this very time. Just imagine how frightened she must have been as she wondered if her baby was a girl or a boy. Finally, the day came when she delivered a boy—"a goodly child" according to Exodus 2:2. Jochebed hid him three months. The roll call of the faithful declares, "By faith Moses, when he was born, was hid three months of his parents, because they saw he was a proper child; and they were not afraid of the king's commandment" (Hebrews 11:23). Why did Jochebed hide her son? Not only did she love him, but she believed he was special to God. She risked her life to protect him.

Keep in mind that Jochebed was a Levite, and it is almost certain that she had asked God for His guidance and protection as she worked to prepare a little boat for her baby Moses. She set in motion what she hoped would be a plan for his future.

> And when she could not longer hide him, she took for him an ark [a box or small container] of bulrushes [papyrus], and daubed it with slime and with pitch [tree resin], and put the child therein; and she laid it in the flags [irises or cattails] by the river's brink (Exodus 2:3).

The baby Moses must have had a special appearance or manner because we're told that he was a "proper child." Perhaps this special quality was the reason that Jochebed could no longer hide him after he reached three months of age.

Jochebed did not abandon Moses in the river, for "his sister stood afar off" to see what would be done to him (Exodus 2:4). Did God tell Jochebed to leave Moses in the river? Did she know that the king's daughter made a habit of bathing there? The Bible does not say. We do know, however, "that all things work together for good to them that love God" (Romans 8:28). I'm certain that Jochebed loved her child and, as a Levite, she loved God. We know that she showed extraordinary self-control and courage when she placed him in the water that day.

A Flawless Plan

As Miriam watched, Pharaoh's daughter, with her attendants, came to the Nile to bathe. Almost immediately, the Egyptian princess saw the little boat and sent one of her maids into the water to fetch it. Upon opening the ark, she knew the baby was a Hebrew (Exodus 2:5–7).

What happened next is too perfect for mere coincidence. God's hand of providence arranged for Miriam to step up at that very moment and inquire of the princess regarding a wet-nurse for the baby. Of course, the wet-nurse Miriam recommended was the baby's own mother, Jochebed! When the princess agreed, the plan was set flawlessly in place.

Miriam hurried away and returned with Jochebed who graciously agreed to be the nurse for the baby. Pharaoh's daughter provided for the family while Jochebed fed and cared for Moses. Bible scholars believe his mother kept Moses for about three years, since most Jewish mothers waited until that time to wean their children. Keep in mind that in addition to physically caring for the baby, Jochebed and Amram had the opportunity to teach him about God and their Hebrew customs. They must have done an excellent job, since Moses remembered what he had been taught over forty years later.

> HER LOVE EMPOWERED HER TO HAND MOSES OVER TO ANOTHER.

What was the true measure of Jochebed's temperance? That is revealed in what happened after the baby was weaned. Instead of hoping Pharaoh's daughter would forget about the baby she had found in the river or running away to hide, Jochebed gave the baby back to the princess. Imagine how she must have struggled to control her maternal instincts and love.

Nothing is more foreign to the maternal instinct than for a mother to give up a child she has born from her own body. Jochebed used more prudence and temperance in her actions than many courageous men of war could have mustered. Her love for her child and her love for God and His plan for her son empowered her to hand Moses over to the princess. She showed true self-control when she did that. What an example for us today!

QUESTIONS ABOUT YOUR PRESCRIPTION

1. What is temperance?

2. Discuss two areas of your life in which you are careful to practice temperance. Why?

3. What does the following statement mean to you? "Christianity has not so much been tried and found wanting, as been found difficult and left untried."

4. Why do you think Vashti refused to go to her husband's banquet?

5. What thoughts might Vashti have been having?

6. Vashti disobeyed her husband to uphold a higher principle. Were her actions acceptable to God? Why or why not?

7. How did Jochebed figure into God's plan for Moses and the Hebrews?

8. Read Numbers 12:1–16 and tell why Miriam had a disagreement with Moses some eighty years after she cared for him as a baby. Had she followed her mother's example, how might the events of Numbers 12 played out?

9. From reading the story of Jochebed and Moses, would you say that the teaching a very young child receives is important later in life? How are Bible classes and religious training at home valuable to a child three or four years old?

10. Why can't a person be a true Christian without having temperance?

FURTHER RESEARCH

∽ Discuss an instance in the life of Christ when He was the embodiment of temperance? (Hint: It had something to do with a desert.)

∽ List other women in the Bible who are examples of temperate living.

Patience

THE DAILY PRACTICE

PRESCRIPTION

And beside this, giving all diligence, add to your faith virtue; and to virtue knowledge; and to knowledge temperance; and to temperance patience; *and to patience godliness; and to godliness brotherly kindness; and to brotherly kindness charity* (2 Peter 1:5–7).

PHYSICIAN'S INSTRUCTIONS

Wherefore seeing we also are compassed about with so great a cloud of witnesses, let us lay aside every weight, and the sin which doth so easily beset us, and let us run with patience the race that is set before us (Hebrews 12:1).

DAILY DOSE

2 Peter 3:9	Romans 2:4
Hebrews 10:36	James 5:7
1 Timothy 6:11	

What Is Patience?

In spite of the old joke, "Lord, give me patience and give it to me right now," patience has to be achieved in a steady progression rather than overnight. Some consider patience to be the passive waiting for something to happen. However, the word *patience* in the New Testament is translated from action words similar to the phrase in our "Physicians Instructions," "run with patience the race that is set before us."

Let's take a minute and look at patience, along with some similar words.

- *Patience*—an abiding under: that is, withstanding the temptation to quit when things don't go your way. Further, patience is the quality that does not surrender to circumstances or succumb under trial. It is the opposite of despondency and is associated with hope. It is never used as a quality of God.

- *Longsuffering*—literally, a long temper. Even though God is never described as patient, He is often said to be longsuffering. He allows us to continue sinning without striking us dead, but He never has a problem "bearing up under" stress Satan tries to place on Him.

- *Forbearance*—a holding back, a delay of punishment; a dispensing of wrath that must be exercised unless the violator accepts the condition of terms set by the one violated.

What is he best way to understand the patience Peter prescribes as a part of a Christian's character? Let's look to God's Word for examples. God is longsuffering. Throughout the history of civilization, He has been most longsuffering in regards to man's mistakes and sins. If we, as Christians, can understand a tiny fraction of God's ability to be longsuffering, we will be much better able to exercise the kind of patience Peter has set for us.

The Bible is filled with examples of the longsuffering of God. Here are two examples.

ଏଓ "The Lord is not slack concerning his promise, as some men count slackness; but is longsuffering to us-ward, not willing that any should perish, but that all should come to repentance" (2 Peter 3:9).

ଏଓ "Or despisest thou the riches of his goodness and forbearance and longsuffering; not knowing that the goodness of God leadeth thee to repentance?" (Romans 2:4.)

In these verses we see God's exercising forbearance with us—being longsuffering—because He wants us to be saved eternally. If God will do that, we surely should be able to exercise patience—bear up under—any difficulties our enemies, or even our friends, put in our way.

Does everyone need patience? Hebrews 10:36 states, "For ye have need of patience, that, after ye have done the will of God, ye might receive the promise." And James says, "Be patient therefore, brethren, unto the coming of the Lord" (James 5:7). Finally, Paul echoes Peter's prescription for our souls when he says, "But you, O man of God, flee these things and pursue righteousness, godliness, faith, love, patience, gentleness" (1 Timothy 6:11); and in Galatians 5:22 he says, "But the fruit of the Spirit is love, joy, peace, longsuffering, gentleness, goodness, faith, meekness, temperance: against such there is no law."

Patience: The Daily Practice—How Can I Develop It?

Patience is yet another quality that must be learned. No one is born patient. If you do not believe that, think of how a baby or small child acts when she is hungry or tired. She doesn't exhibit an inkling of patience. As she succumbs to the desire to eat, her screams can be heard several doors down the street. Children must be taught to practice patience. Most of us avoid adults who haven't learned patience. Granted, some may gain a larger measure of it in a shorter amount of time than others, but everyone has the capacity for some measure of patience.

1. *Recognize God's power and His love for us.* In fact, we should be joyful that God strengthens us for His purpose: "Strengthened with all might, according to his glorious power, unto all patience and longsuffering with joyfulness" (Colossians 1:11). The knowledge that God is "waiting in the wings" to give each of us a mere portion of His strength and patience should be a cause for happiness for every Christian.

   Patiently enduring life's problems is something for which God will reward us. James encourages us when he says, "Knowing this, that the trying of your faith worketh patience. But let patience have her perfect work, that ye may be perfect and entire, wanting nothing" (James 1:3–4). We become more patient by being tested.

2. *Trust God's goodness.* For some, this is one of the most difficult aspects of being a Christian. Too often, we are inclined to jump in and try to solve everything ourselves. Perhaps it's the caretaker in us or it may be an issue of control. "Letting go and letting God" is an admonition that's often difficult to follow. Let's act as if we really believe this verse: "And we know that all things work together for good to them that love God, to them who are the called according to his purpose" (Romans 8:28).

3. *Rest and wait for God.* It is hard for some Christians to accept that God accomplishes His will in His time, not ours.

This resting and waiting is another excellent way of learning patience. The psalmist said,

> Rest in the Lord and wait patiently for him: fret not thyself because of him who prospereth in his way, because of the man who bringeth wicked devices to pass. Cease from anger, and forsake wrath: fret not thyself in any wise to do evil. For evildoers shall be cut off: but those that wait upon the Lord, they shall inherit the earth (Psalm 37:7–9).

4. *Look forward to Christ's return.* This is the practice exercise for patience that every Christian should enjoy: simply looking forward to Christ's return. James phrased it simply and beautifully this way,

> Be patient therefore, brethren, unto the coming of the Lord. Behold, the husbandman waiteth for the precious fruit of the earth, and hath long patience for it, until he receive the early and latter rain. Be ye also patient; stablish your hearts: for the coming of the Lord draweth nigh (James 5:7–8).

Adverse Side Effects of Patience

∞ *Complacency*—Christians who work hard to be patient might run the risk of becoming complacent. Complacency is "a feeling of contentment or self-satisfaction, especially when coupled with an unawareness of danger, trouble, or controversy." Complacent people usually accept the present state of affairs with no resistance. We know that God does not mean for us to become complacent in our Christian lives. Complacency can grow out of a false security that creates a lukewarm faith. Revelation 3:15 states, "I know thy works, that thou art neither cold nor hot: I would thou wert cold or hot." This sense of false security is not a result of an active Christian patience because

Peter tells us to "be sober, be vigilant; because your adversary the devil, as a roaring lion, walketh about, seeking whom he may devour" (1 Peter 5:8).

◈ *Weakness*—Patient people run the risk of being viewed by others as weak or passive. A weak person is one who lacks the strength to act, while a passive person isolates herself from the action. Both of these people may be motivated by fear of the consequences of their actions. This is not true of a genuinely patient person. Patience is dynamic and forward-thinking and is a part of the Lord's own character,

> The Lord is not slack concerning his promise, as some men count slackness; but is longsuffering to us-ward, not willing that any should perish, but that all should come to repentance (2 Peter 3:9).

Weakness drives people to quick reactions while patient people know that they must look at the "big picture." We should always remember that we must "let patience have her perfect work, that ye may be perfect and entire, lacking nothing" (James 1:4).

WOMEN OF PATIENCE

Mrs. Noah

Our first example of a patient woman is Noah's wife. Her history is found in Genesis 6–9. We know that she had a righteous husband, just and perfect in his generation, who "walked with God" (Genesis 6:9). Knowing this, we can be sure that Mrs. Noah was treated well and cared for by her husband. We also know that she, herself, was righteous because she was one of only eight souls saved from the flood (Genesis 8:16).

We can assume that Noah's wife faithfully helped him during several hundred years of farming (Genesis 5:29). The Bible tells us she was with him when he preached righteousness to a wicked world for over a hundred years (2 Peter 2:5). Just imagine the atmosphere during the time when Noah was preaching. Every "imagination of the thoughts of his [mankind's] heart was only evil continually" (Genesis 6:5). She and her husband and family were surrounded by adulterers, murderers, child molesters, rapists, robbers, and all other kinds of depraved and sinful people. Mrs. Noah probably lived in fear of physical attack—and worse—every day of her existence during this time. Yet she stood by her husband and patiently supported him.

HER FAMILY WAS SURROUNDED BY DEPRAVED AND SINFUL PEOPLE.

Mrs. Noah could have doubted Noah's predictions because, so far as we know, it had never rained on earth at that time (Genesis 2:5–6). But she didn't. She could have thought that boat building and preaching were taking too much time. But she didn't. Through patience and faith, Mrs. Noah worked with her husband in an attempt to turn wicked mankind from their sins so they could be saved. She believed that God could and would save them as He had promised.

As the time of the flood drew nearer, maybe Mrs. Noah helped her husband prepare the animals for the voyage. Keep in mind, that was no small task. The ark measured 450 feet long, 75 feet wide, and 45 feet high. Modern scholars have estimated that the ark would be equivalent in volume to 522 standard American railroad stock cars, each of which can hold 240 sheep. This means that the ark itself held about 25,000 animals with enough space left over for enough food and supplies to last a year!

Ending and Beginning

Besides patience, Mrs. Noah must have had the ability to envision a future unlike anything she had ever seen. At the end of his preaching, Noah knew that he and his family would be the only people saved from the flood (Genesis 6:13). Through her faith and patience, Mrs. Noah had to cope with the idea of living in a world that was inhabited by only her family and to realize that they would become the ancestors of everyone yet to be born on the earth. Only a woman with a strong faith and a powerfully patient nature could have handled that realization.

Perhaps the most trying time for Noah's wife was the year that she and her family spent on the ark with all the animals. Just imagine the smells and sounds that were almost constant! Add the fact that there were only eight people to feed, water, and clean up after all those thousands of animals. Then factor in Mrs. Noah's duties as the matriarch of the family, shouldering the responsibility to feed, clothe, and monitor the health of her husband, her three sons, and their wives. Most certainly, she was a patient person. There surely was no spare time left to sit around and wait for things to happen! Her patience surely was quiet; her perseverance, steady and constant; and her care, even-tempered.

THIS MATRIARCH SHOULDERED FAMILY RESPONSIBILITY.

The final stage of Mrs. Noah's life began when she left the ark and stepped down among the reminders of all that had been. If ever there was an occasion for fear and doubt to enter her mind, then would have been the time. The Bible doesn't tell us what she and her husband thought, but it does say that "Noah built an altar unto the Lord; and . . . offered burnt offerings on the altar" (Genesis 8:20). After all their trials, Noah's and his wife's hearts remained with God. This fact and

Mrs. Noah's selfless support of her husband make her a great example of the kind of patience Peter prescribed.

Elizabeth, Mother of John the Baptizer

In Luke 1:5–80 we find another excellent example of the type of patience that Peter prescribes. Elizabeth, mother of John the baptizer was a cousin of Mary, the mother of Jesus. She was the wife of Zacharias, a Jewish priest. Both she and her husband were of the tribe of Levi.

Theirs was a good life for good people: "And they were both righteous before God, walking in all the commandments and ordinances of the Lord blameless." However, there was one problem that must have seemed insurmountable to them— Elizabeth was barren and past childbearing age, "And they had no child, because that Elisabeth was barren, and they both were now well stricken in years" (Luke 1:7).

What characterized society of Elizabeth's day? Women were expected to have many children. Being childless was a cause of shame for a wife and a reflection of dishonor for her husband. No doubt, Elizabeth had patiently prayed for a child for many years. Throughout this time she may have wondered why God had not seen fit to give her a baby, but she didn't question Him. She waited patiently and continued to live a blameless life with her husband. Certainly, she behaved perfectly in a very difficult and potentially hurtful situation. Even so, the townsfolk probably labeled her "cursed by God."

Shame and Dishonor Removed

The Bible tells us that it was Zacharias's turn to "burn incense when he went into the temple of the Lord." As he was completing his tasks, the angel of the Lord appeared to him beside the incense burner. Imagine how Zacharias must have felt! Here he was, doing his usual job on an ordinary day, and suddenly an angel appears—not just any angel but Gabriel, a special angel of the Lord. This is the same heavenly being and direct representative of God, who announced Samson's birth in Judges 13. He would also speak to Mary concerning the birth of Jesus (Luke 1:26–37); to Joseph (Matthew 2:13); to the shepherds (Luke 2:9); and to Philip (Acts 8:26). He is also the one who freed Peter from prison (Acts 12:7). He carried God's messages to many other Bible characters.

Naturally, Zacharias was very startled and afraid when he glimpsed the angel. But his fear was turned to joy and amazement when the angel told him that Elizabeth would soon have a baby who would "be great in the sight of the Lord" and "be filled with the Holy Ghost, even from his mother's womb" (Luke 1: 12–15).

Zacharias suddenly appears completely human when he asks the angel, "Whereby shall I know this? for I am an old man, and my wife well stricken in years?" How many of us would have asked the same question? Most, I imagine. But because Zacharias did question the angel's statements, Gabriel caused Zacharias to become unable to speak "until the day that these things shall be performed, because thou believest not my words, which shall be fulfilled in their season."

MOTHER-TO-BE ELIZABETH WAS "WELL STRICKEN IN YEARS."

Not long afterward, Elizabeth, who could have been eighty or more years of age—we are only told that she was "well stricken in years"—became pregnant. Again, her patience must have been sorely tested by the townspeople whose questions and wondering glances met her everywhere she went. The Bible says she hid herself away for five months, saying, "Thus hath the Lord dealt with me in the days wherein he looked on me, to take away my reproach among men."

When Elizabeth was six months pregnant, she had a very special guest. When her cousin, Mary of Nazareth, entered her house, Elizabeth was given a favor so special that no other person had ever received it. She was the first person to have the privilege of calling Mary's unborn child "Lord." She obviously was able to recognize the deity of Mary's baby because her own baby was "filled with the Holy Ghost, even from his mother's womb." Perhaps this wonderful favor was part of Elizabeth's reward for her enduring patience.

QUESTIONS ABOUT YOUR PRESCRIPTION

1. Define patience.

2. Are you a patient person? Why or why not?

3. Explain why you think Peter included patience in his list of qualities that are necessary to strengthen our souls.

4. Tell about a time when your patience was tested. How did you feel? What did you do?

5. Noah's wife had many challenges that required a great deal of patience. Discuss two of them.

6. Do you think Noah could have completed his job as well as he did if his wife had not been with him? Why or why not?

7. Zacharias' question to Gabriel was certainly a human one. Do you think his doubt made him any less righteous in God's sight? Why or why not?

8. Elizabeth is a good example of godly patience. List some examples of her patience.

9. Teaching and leaning patience are difficult tasks. What are some things that can help us in this process?

10. Describe the kind of patience Elizabeth and Zacharias needed in raising John. Read Luke 1:15–17 and think about what the angel said about him before he was born. What are some of the challenges of raising a gifted or special child?

FURTHER RESEARCH

- Do you know any childless couples? How might you encourage them?

- Was Sarah, Abraham's wife, a patient woman? Why or why not? (Genesis 16.)

- Who do you think was more patient—Mary or Martha? (Luke 10:38–42; John 11:1–45; John 12:1–8.) Why?

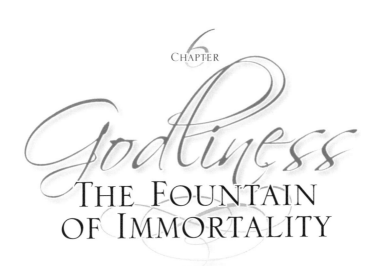

CHAPTER 6

Godliness

THE FOUNTAIN
OF IMMORTALITY

PRESCRIPTION

And beside this, giving all diligence, add to your faith virtue; and to virtue knowledge; And to knowledge temperance; and to temperance patience; and to patience godliness; And to godliness brotherly kindness; and to brotherly kindness charity (2 Peter 1: 5 –7).

PHYSICIAN'S INSTRUCTIONS

But refuse profane and old wives' fables, and exercise thyself rather unto godliness (1 Timothy 4:7).

DAILY DOSE

1 Timothy 4:7	1 Timothy 3:16
1 Timothy 4:8	2 Peter 1:3
Hebrews 5:13–14	

What Is Godliness?

Godliness is "conforming to the laws and wishes of God" and "striving to be more like God each day." The Greek word from which godliness comes means "piety, devotion, or a disposition of God-likeness." Sometimes a medication bears the doctor's instructions: "Drink plenty of water and take capsules with food." Similarly, godliness is powered by large amounts of study and of prayer.

Just as we must be educated in what not to do for our physical health, so Paul instructs Timothy: "Refuse profane and old wives' fables" (1 Timothy 4:7). When we open our ears to the teachings of humans, we are closing the door on God's way. What is difficult to understand about the word *refuse?* To quote a popular ad slogan: "Just say no." Clean your house of human error and foolishness such as astrology, mythology, numerology, and other theories, and "exercise thyself rather unto godliness" (1 Timothy 4:7). Achieving godliness involves active participation, much like physical exercise. Is a once-a-week exercise program sufficient to keep us spiritually fit? Any trainer would answer with an emphatic no!

CLEAN YOUR HOUSE OF HUMAN ERROR AND FOOLISHNESS.

Paul calls godliness a mystery: "And without controversy great is the mystery of godliness" (1 Timothy 3:16). My research turned up another interpretation of the Greek word for *mystery:* "that which was formerly obscured, but which has now been announced through the gospel of Christ. It has to do with the unfolding of the heavenly scheme of salvation." This implies that godliness is the continued progress toward becoming Christ-like. The trait of godliness was shrouded or mysterious to those who lived before Christ's birth, but now it is clear in the Gospels and other writings of the apostles. We are the beneficiaries of this revealed mystery!

In comparing the physical with the spiritual, Paul told Timothy: "For bodily exercise profiteth little: but godliness is profitable unto all things, having promise of the life that now is, and of that which is to come" (1 Timothy 4:8). "All things" leaves nothing out. There is not an area of life that is not enhanced by the trait of godliness. More important, without godliness, we have no promise of life in heaven. The "godliness pill" is a big pill to swallow, but a very necessary one.

Paul warns Christians to withdraw themselves from "perverse disputings of men of corrupt minds, and destitute of the truth, supposing that gain is godliness" (1 Timothy 6:5). He continues: "But godliness with contentment is great gain" (1 Timothy 6:6). In other words, Christians should stay away from those who have evil minds and lying tongues, whose only objective is to gain money and goods. Godliness with contentment—a satisfied mind—is worth more than anyone's earthy treasures.

Godliness—How Can I Develop It?

ᕔ *Discipline.* Paul told Timothy to "exercise thyself rather unto godliness" (1 Timothy 4:7). Discipline means work and sustained daily effort. Exercise involves training and discipline. Just as an athlete eats correctly, sleeps sufficiently, and trains to reach a goal, a Christian woman should discipline herself to become more godly each day. Keep in mind that Paul had been to Greece and probably had seen the athletes as they trained and exercised. He even used the same kind of athletic comparison about himself in 2 Timothy 2:7–8:

> I have fought a good fight, I have finished my course, I have kept the faith: henceforth there is laid up for me a crown of righteousness, which the Lord, the righteous

judge, shall give me at that day: and not to me only, but unto all them also that love his appearing.

൦ᴧ *Daily Bible study.* Have a set place and time for daily prayer and meditation. A godly woman will strive to reflect God in her life. When she looks into the mirror of God's Word, her soul will be fair to behold! Godliness won't come in an instant or even in a year. Make it your goal to live each day with the thought: "What can I do, say, or think that will make me more like God and His Son, Jesus?" Regular meditation enables the Christian to say no to self and yes to Christ every day. Soon worldly habits and actions are replaced by godly ones.

The Hebrew Christians were chastised because they were merely standing still in the Lord. Sure, they had obeyed the gospel, but that was where their activity ended.

> For when for the time ye ought to be teachers, ye have need that one teach you again which be the first principles of the oracles of God; and are become such as have need of milk, and not of strong meat. For every one that useth milk is unskillful in the word of righteousness: for he is a babe (Hebrews 5:12–14).

They were babies, with no knowledge of God's Word, and no plan to become more godly each day.

൦ᴧ *Encouragement.* Keep in mind that you are not alone in striving for godliness, but " it is God which worketh in you both to will and to do of his good pleasure" (Philippians 2:13). Romans 8:31 asks us, "If God be for us, who can be against us?" So often we women are busy with so many urgent and unimportant things that we fail to tap into our encouraging words! How sad that our Father is waiting to comfort and encourage us, but we do not take time to allow it! How can we manage life alone? We need His help to add godliness to our Christian characters.

Adverse Side Effects of Godliness

Do you think you have godliness? You reason that you are studying your Bible every day with prayer and meditation. You are disciplined. And then, without warning, you suffer side effects from your godliness prescription. They can cause a great deal of trouble if left untreated.

அ *Conceit*—This ailment can be a "silent killer" if not caught early. Of course, we should be conscious of our progress toward godliness, and we should feel pleased with ourselves as we mature and grow. The problem comes when we allow this pleasure with ourselves to ripen into full-blown conceit or "an excessively favorable opinion of one's own ability, importance, or wit." Conceit turns the focus from God back to us; that is unacceptable. Paul is referring to conceit when he states, "Let nothing be done through strife or vainglory; but in lowliness of mind let each esteem other better than themselves" (Philippians 2:3). Solomon also warned against it: "Answer a fool according to his folly, lest he be wise in his own conceit" (Proverbs 26:5).

அ *Narrow-mindedness*—Narrow-mindedness results when a Christian begins to think that her godliness is complete and that her way of living is the only acceptable way. Narrow-minded people are not willing to accept the opinions and ideas of others even if there's a possibility that they are correct. Narrow-mindedness can easily turn into conceit and self-importance, so be very watchful of its warning signs. Christ addressed narrow-minded people in Matthew 7:1: "Judge not, that ye be not judged." And again in Matthew 7:4, "Or how wilt thou say to thy brother, Let me pull out the mote out of thine eye; and, behold, a beam is in thine own eye?" Always be on guard for narrow-mindedness in your journey toward godliness.

WOMEN OF GODLINESS

Mary and Martha of Bethany

Jesus loved Mary, Martha, and Lazarus of Bethany. Their home was one of a very few that Christ visited for relaxation and fellowship. Mary and Martha had seen Christ raise Lazarus from the dead after he had been in the tomb four days. They were true believers in Christ's gospel and in His deity. John writes about this family in John 11.

The Scriptures tell us nothing about Martha and Mary except that they were the sisters of Lazarus and that they lived in Bethany. Martha was probably the oldest: "A certain woman named Martha received Him unto her house (Luke 10:38). Whether or not she owned the house, housekeeping and hospitality were very important to Martha. Her warm home must have meant a great deal to Jesus since, in normal circumstances, He had "not where to lay his head" (Matthew 8:20).

JESUS REMINDED HER OF WHAT HINDERS SPIRITUALITY.

Mary and Martha are spoken about together and compared, but both women were godly in their own way. In Luke 10:38–42 we read of Martha, a woman who loved Jesus and wanted everything to be just right for His visit. Imagine her frustration as she hurriedly made preparations for their guest when she observed Mary just sitting and listening to Jesus talk. When Martha appealed to Jesus for help, He reminded her that she was permitting her outward activities and responsibilities to hinder her spirituality (Luke 10:41).

Whatever You Ask, God Will Give

When Lazarus became very seriously ill, the two sisters sent for Jesus immediately. When He did finally arrive, Martha was the first to greet him: "Lord, if thou hadst been here, my brother had not died. But I know, that even now, whatsoever thou wilt ask of God, God will give it thee" (John 11:21–22).

It was then that Jesus uttered one of the most important and profound statements of all time,

> I am the resurrection and the life; he that believeth in Me, though he were dead, yet shall he live, and whosoever believeth in Me shall never die. Believeth thou this? (John 11: 25–26.)

By asking Martha if she believed He could save her, Jesus gave her the utmost privilege of being the first woman to make the statement that all Christians must make if they are to be in complete obedience to God's will—that Jesus Christ is the Son of God.

Jesus did raise Lazarus from the dead and the sisters rejoiced! Martha truly is a good example for us to follow because she was able to keep in memory everything she had been taught about Christ and God. Martha believed completely in Christ's power to save her brother and herself. Her attitude and good deeds demonstrate her humanity and her pursuit of godliness.

Mary Sat Still in the House

Mary's personality was quite different from Martha's. Scripture tells us, "[Martha] had a sister called Mary, which also sat at Jesus' feet, and heard his word" (Luke 10:39). Mary was a good listener, quieter and more contemplative than Martha. Truly, they are the biblical examples of the type A and B personalities! Like Martha, type A folks are hard workers who are often preoccupied with schedules and the speed of their performance, while type B people are more creative, imaginative, and philosophical.

Mary was enthralled by the words of Jesus. He spoke unlike anyone she had ever heard. She knew He was telling her about the way to eternal life. Even when Martha asked Jesus why she was sitting and not working, Mary did not respond angrily. Her nature was very much like her Savior's which was prophesied in Isaiah 53:7: "He was oppressed, and he was afflicted, yet he opened not his mouth." Mary's temperament was godly.

OUT OF LOVE AND DEVOTION, SHE DID WHAT SHE COULD.

Mary offered Jesus her greatest devotion and service. She joined with Him in quiet talks and devotionals away from the noisy crowds that followed Him. When Martha questioned this, He said, "But one thing is needful: and Mary hath chosen that good part, which shall not be taken away from her."

Mary was a very loving sister to Martha and Lazarus. When Lazarus died, Mary did not strike out at God and scream. Rather she "sat still in the house." She dealt quietly with her grief. Again, we see evidence of her desire to be godly in her actions. When she left the house and came to Jesus, He saw her weeping over her brother. So deeply affected by their brother's death and the sorrow that was so evident in both of the sisters, Jesus wept.

Finally, we see Mary at the house of Simon the leper (Mark 14:3; John 12:3). She evidently knew the time of Christ's death was very near because she "took a pound of ointment of spikenard, very costly, and anointed the feet of Jesus, and wiped his feet with her hair: and the house was filled with the odor of the ointment." Her love and devotion for the Savior was so great that she did what she could—she helped to prepare Him for His burial (John 12:7). Mary was a woman who worked each day to become more like her God and Savior. Her devotion and desire to be godly was so wonderful that Jesus said, "Verily I say unto you, Wheresoever this gospel shall be preached in the whole world, there shall also this, that this woman hath done, be told for a memorial of her" (Matthew 26:13).

QUESTIONS ABOUT YOUR PRESCRIPTION

1. What is godliness?

2. Are the components of godliness a mystery to us today? Explain your answer.

3. Is godliness any more or less important than any other of the qualities that Peter discusses in 2 Peter 1:5–11? Why or why not?

4. Martha told Jesus that her brother would have lived if He had been there. Was Martha whining and rebuking Jesus for not being there, or was she showing her absolute confidence in Jesus and His power to save? Defend your answer.

5. List Martha's traits that resembled those of the virtuous woman in Proverbs 31.

6. Can a person be a perfectionist—as it appears Martha was—and still be a Christian?

7. Do you think Mary routinely left Martha with all the work? Why or why not?

8. How did Jesus help each sister with her sorrow over Lazarus's death?

9. Comment on the phrase "Mary sat still in the house." What are the benefits of sitting still?

10. Why do you suppose Jesus said Mary's gift would be remembered wherever the gospel is preached?

FURTHER RESEARCH

∞ Make a list of godly women and men that you know.

∞ What characteristics do godly people have in common?

CHAPTER 7

Kindness
THE HEALING OIL

PRESCRIPTION

And beside this, giving all diligence, add to your faith virtue; and to virtue knowledge; and to knowledge temperance; and to temperance patience; and to patience godliness; and to godliness brotherly kindness; and to brotherly kindness charity (2 Peter 1:5–7).

PHYSICIAN'S INSTRUCTIONS

And be ye kind one to another, tenderhearted, forgiving one another, even as God for Christ's sake hath forgiven you (Ephesians 4:32).

DAILY DOSE

Luke 6:35	Romans 12:10
John 13:34	Romans 8:29
Matthew 22:39	

What Is Kindness?

Although God expects Christians to be kind to all people (Luke 6:35), our "Prescription" specifically mentions "brotherly kindness" as a quality we all should nurture. One can be kind to strangers and pets; however, brotherly kindness carries a more significant meaning. Brotherly kindness is from two Greek words: *phileo*, 'love' and *adelphos*, 'brother.' The resulting word, *philadelphia*, literally means "the love of brothers." As it is used in the New Testament, *philadelphia* describes the love Christians should have for other Christians. Romans 12:10 says, "Be kindly affectioned one to another with brotherly love; in honor preferring one another." This admonition means that we should try to outdo one another in showing respect! How will this attitude change your relationship with your sisters and brothers? Brotherly kindness implies a sense of family to be shared with other members of the Lord's church.

TRY TO OUTDO ONE ANOTHER IN SHOWING RESPECT!

Jesus explained the depth of love we should have for our brothers and sisters in Christ when He said, "A new commandment I give unto you, That ye love one another; as I have loved you, that ye also love one another" (John 13:34). This type of love carries with it a much greater responsibility than merely allowing a stranger to go ahead of you in a checkout line or giving a stray puppy some food. When we consider His sacrifice for us, then our own pitiful excuses for being unkind are pale with insignificance.

Brotherly kindness involves a heartfelt commitment to each other with the knowledge that we, as members of the Lord's church, are bound together with a very special tie. We should treat each other with more affection and concern than we offer our friends and acquaintances in the world. If we sincerely wish to attain the level of Christian development that Peter speaks about in the "Prescription" text, we must work to develop Christ-like kindness. After all, Paul tells us we should be "conformed to the image of [God's] Son, that . . .

[we] might be the firstborn among many brethren" (Romans 8:29). Also, Christ instructed His followers to love their neighbors as themselves (Matthew 22:39).

How difficult is it to show kindness to those who love us and treat us with respect? The real test comes when we feel mistreated. A sister may make an insensitive remark or a brother might ignore you. Peter was inspired by the Holy Spirit to include brotherly kindness as one prescription for abundant living. Just as with the other qualities we have studied, so it is with brotherly kindness. Adding it to our characters is not just a suggestion; it is a commandment. God expects us to obey it.

Cultivating Kindness—How Can I Develop It?

1. *Remember whose you are.* Perhaps this is the most fundamental method of developing brotherly kindness. Christians are the "elect of God," the people whom God chose—His children. If we are unkind to each other, how can we hope to convince the world that they should be following Christ? Colossians 3:12 states, "Put on therefore, as God's elect, holy and beloved, a heart of compassion, kindness, lowliness, meekness, longsuffering" (ASV).

   God showed kindness toward mankind by sending Jesus. Paul says,

   > And [God] hath raised us up together, and made us sit together in heavenly places in Christ Jesus: that in the ages to come He might shew the exceeding riches of His grace in His kindness toward us through Christ Jesus (Ephesians 2:6–7).

   In Titus 3:4 he continues to stress the fact that the kindness of God is the reason we have Jesus Christ, "But after that the kindness and love of God our Savior toward man appeared."

2. *Follow Christ's example in kindness.* Paul says, "And be ye kind one to another, tenderhearted, forgiving one another, even as God for Christ's sake hath forgiven you" (Ephesians 4:32). Christ was kind to all people, not just those who were kind to Him. Consequently, we certainly have a high standard to follow, don't we? Remember His interaction with children, victims of disease, false accusers, women of questionable reputation, Judas, and even Peter himself!

In Galatians 5:22–23, Paul listed brotherly kindness as a fruit of the spirit. As do literal fruits, kindness develops through a growth process. It begins with a seed and finally yields mature, loving Christians. Along with all the qualities advocated by Peter in 2 Peter 1:5–11, brotherly kindness must be cultivated, promoted, and fostered. It ripens over time with care.

3. *Study the Scriptures.* The Bible has answers to all things that pertain to life and godliness. When we have problems with our brothers or sisters, do we go to the gossip tree or to the Scriptures? Why not look for the soft answer to turn away wrath? Practice peace, as Jesus did, by asking questions rather than by making harsh condemning statements.

Notice the following admonitions from Jesus and the apostle Paul:

> Ye have heard that it hath been said, Thou shalt love thy neighbour, and hate thine enemy. But I say unto you, Love your enemies, bless them that curse you, do good to them that hate you, and pray for them which despitefully use you, and persecute you; That ye may

KINDNESS — THE HEALING OIL

be the children of your Father which is in heaven:
(Matthew 5:43–45).

And let us not be weary in well doing: for in due season
we shall reap, if we faint not. As we have therefore opportunity, let us do good unto all men, especially unto
them who are of the household of faith (Galatians
6:9–10).

From these examples, can you see that doing good and being kind are essential Christian virtues?

4. *Spend time with the church.* Since the church is God's people, how can we show kindness for our fellow Christians
unless we get to know them? Three hours a week in the
church house is simply not enough time to truly get to
know and love each other. Many churches plan opportunities for Christians to play and work together. As with an
earthly family, eating together is an excellent way to inter-
twine lives. It's also a great way to observe opportunities
to be kind: Does a young family need a break? Does an
older member need a visit? Does a grieving widow need a
listening ear? As our relationships with fellow Christians
grow, so will our chances to follow Christ's lead. The more
we try to be kind to one another, the more Christ-like we
will become. This will, in turn, lead to Christian maturity
as we obey the command, "Let brotherly love continue"
(Hebrews 13:1).

Adverse Side Effects of Brotherly Kindness

  Someone will take advantage of you. Worldly people sometimes view kind people as weak and gullible, but they do
not understand the higher call of the Christian. A woman
who chooses to follow Christ's example will run the risk
of this side effect—her acquaintances might consider her

weak and try to take advantage of her. Beware of that obstacle, but do not let it hinder your attitude. After all, you answer to a higher power! Follow the Holy Spirit's instructions:

> Let nothing be done through strife or vainglory; but in lowliness of mind let each esteem other better than themselves. Look not every man on his own things, but every man also on the things of others (Philippians 2:3–4).

You will be taken for granted. Have you ever felt taken for granted? I'm sure you have. Anyone who practices being kind has had that experience many times. Our human nature tends to seek assistance from those who have expressed kindness in the past. But a problem arises when one continues to seek assistance from the same person or group. It is easy to impose on a sister or brother in Christ, and it is just as easy to become the person who is being imposed upon or taken for granted. Since Paul tells us that we must be "giving thanks always for all things unto God and the Father in the name of our Lord Jesus Christ" (Ephesians 5:20), it is reasonable to conclude that we must never take God, Christ, or our fellow Christians for granted when they continue to do good to us. As in the previous example, a Christian woman must be on guard to expect this side effect and persevere in her path of kindness in spite of the risk of being taken for granted.

WOMEN OF KINDNESS

Dorcas

One outstanding example of a Christian who understood the true meaning of brotherly kindness is found in Acts 9:36–43. Dorcas (also known as Tabitha) lived in Joppa near the present-day capital of Israel, Tel-Aviv. She was known for her good works and almsdeeds or gifts given to benefit the poor. She obviously knew "that they which have believed in God might be careful to maintain good works" (Titus 3:8). She enjoyed making and giving items to her brethren and to the poor.

Dorcas was probably converted by someone who had been in Jerusalem on that first Pentecost after the resurrection of Christ. We know that many churches were established in Judea, Galilee, and Samaria. The mention of saints, along with calling Dorcas a disciple, makes it certain that there was a congregation of the Lord in Joppa. At that time, the churches in that area were enjoying a time of peace and growth:

> Then had the churches rest throughout all Judaea and Galilee and Samaria, and were edified; and walking in the fear of the Lord, and in the comfort of the Holy Ghost, were multiplied (Acts 9:31).

Sadly, in the midst of her benevolence projects, Dorcas became ill and died. Fellow Christians prepared her body for burial. Part of that preparation involved washing her body with warm water with the hope of reviving her. Since bathing her had no such effect, her friends knew she was dead. Later, when Peter raised her up, their attempts could be used to dispute any assertion that she was merely sleeping.

Some of the disciples in Joppa knew Peter was nearby in Lydda, about nine miles away. They sent an urgent plea for him to come quickly to minister to Dorcas. No doubt they had heard that Peter had healed Aeneas in Lydda and prayed that he would do the same thing for Dorcas.

Peter arrived very soon afterward just as Dorcas's friends and fellow Christians were praising her excellent sewing skills and her kind deeds for the poor (v. 39). We know she was loved because "all the widows stood by [Peter] weeping, and shewing the coats and garments which Dorcas made, while she was with them" (Acts 9:39).

The events which followed give us a glimpse of the same Peter who wrote the prescription for mature Christians. This Peter was a man of great knowledge and compassion and very much unlike the young, headstrong fisherman whom Jesus chose to be a "fisher of men" (Mark 1:17). This Peter had been tried and tested. This Peter was filled with the Holy Spirit and with love for God and His Son. This Peter performed miracles.

After seeing the samples of Dorcas's work and hearing about her kindnesses to others, Peter sent everyone out of the room. He then fell to his knees and began to pray. After he had prayed for a while, he turned toward Dorcas and said, "Tabitha, arise." She opened her eyes, and seeing Peter she sat up. The others rushed back into the room and rejoiced when they saw she was alive. Of course, the story of Dorcas's return from the dead spread quickly and "many people believed in the Lord." Dorcas was a Christian woman who truly understood the meaning of brotherly kindness.

Lydia

Lydia's example is found in Acts 16:9–15, 40. It begins with Paul's vision in which a man of Macedonia stands and asks Paul to "come over into Macedonia, and help us." Macedonia was a small republic about the size of Vermont situated in southeastern Europe just above Greece. Paul and his traveling companions—Luke, Timothy, and Silas—immediately went to the city of Philippi in Macedonia.

The group knew Paul's vision was God's way of calling Paul to Philippi to preach the gospel of Christ, so they planned to stay there several days. During that time, they heard about some people who met by the river side on the Sabbath day for prayers and worship. Realizing these were the sort of folks who would probably welcome the good news of Christ, Paul and the others waited until the next Saturday and joined them on the shore.

The worshipers were mostly women and Paul began to teach them about Christ and His church. Lydia paid very close attention to Paul's words. She "and her household" obeyed the gospel. Lydia was the first European Christian.

LYDIA'S WEALTH IS NOT THE REASON SHE IS REMEMBERED TODAY.

Lydia was a special woman. She was originally from Thyatira, a Turkish city east of Philippi. She was a businesswoman, a seller of the purple dye and cloth used to make clothes for royalty and Roman politicians. Purple cloth was very expensive because purple dye had to be extracted, with great difficulty, from a shellfish. Therefore, Lydia was most likely a wealthy woman.

Kindness Persuades

People with money are often memorialized solely because of their riches, but Lydia's wealth is certainly not the reason she is remembered today. There was much more to her character than that. As soon as she was baptized, she told Paul and his companions, "If ye have judged me to be faithful to the Lord, come into my house, and abide there." What a kind and generous offer to a group of men she had known such a short time!

Paul may have been a bit reluctant, even though he and the others were strangers in Philippi with no place to stay. The Bible says, "She constrained [compelled or vigorously encouraged] us." Lydia must have been very persuasive because Paul and the others did stay at her house then, and later, after he and Silas were released from prison.

Lydia practiced the type of brotherly kindness that Peter prescribes for us today. She had the means and the opportunity to do good for God's people, and she took full advantage of it. She could have offered to rent a room for Paul and the others or even ignored their situation completely, but she didn't. Lydia's heart was touched by the gospel of Christ and she wanted to help His cause however she could. She is a sterling example of the kind of person God wants us all to be: "And be ye kind one to another, tenderhearted, forgiving one another, even as God for Christ's sake hath forgiven you" (Ephesians 4:32).

QUESTIONS ABOUT YOUR PRESCRIPTION

1. What is the difference between mere kindness and brotherly kindness?

2. Why is there such a need for brotherly kindness in the world today? Do you think the situation was any different in Peter's time?

3. Do most Christians you know spend very much time together outside worship? If not, what suggestions do you have to make the situation better?

4. What are some ways brotherly kindness might manifest itself among members of the Lord's church?

5. How did Dorcas take advantage of her position as a seamstress?

6. What are some opportunities you have to practice brotherly kindness?

7. What would it be like to be raised from the dead?

8. Read Paul's letter to the Philippians and describe the Christian environment in that congregation where Lydia was a member. Do you think the members there practiced brotherly kindness? Why or why not?

9. Luke says that Lydia and "her household" were baptized (Acts 16:15). Do you think there were any young children in her household? Why or why not?

10. Is it easier to practice brotherly kindness in a small church? Why?

FURTHER RESEARCH

ॐ List and discuss some examples of brotherly kindness in the congregation where you worship?

ॐ List practical ways to prevent someone taking unfair advantage of you, as you strive to practice brotherly kindness.

CHAPTER 8

Charity
THE CHOICE

PRESCRIPTION

And beside this, giving all diligence, add to your faith virtue; and to virtue knowledge; and to knowledge temperance; and to temperance patience; and to patience godliness; and to godliness brotherly kindness; and to brotherly kindness charity *(2 Peter 1:5–7).*

PHYSICIAN'S INSTRUCTIONS

Charity suffereth long, and is kind; charity envieth not; charity vaunteth not itself, is not puffed up, Doth not behave itself unseemly, seeketh not her own, is not easily provoked, thinketh no evil; rejoiceth not in iniquity, but rejoiceth in the truth; Beareth all things, believeth all things, hopeth all things, endureth all things. Charity never faileth . . . (1 Corinthians 13:4–8).

DAILY DOSE

1 Corinthians 13:4–8	1 Peter 4:8
1Timothy 1:5	Colossians 3:14
Romans 14:13–15	

What Is Charity?

In the Bible *charity* means "Christian love—agape." That is exactly the type of love (charity) that Peter prescribes for us. Paul succinctly defines the qualities of charity in our "Physician's Instructions." Read this passage again and underline each quality of love from 1 Corinthians 13:4–8.

Peter and Paul agreed on the kind of love Christians must develop. The qualities of love Peter prescribed for all Christians are set forth in Paul's description of charity.

Paul: Describes Charity	Peter: Prescribes Fruitfulness
Suffers long . . . bears all things . . . endures all things	Patience which means "longsuffering"
Kind	Brotherly kindness
Vaunts not itself . . . does not behave itself unseemly	Virtue
Not puffed up . . . is not easily provoked	Temperance
Thinks no evil; rejoices not in iniquity, but rejoices in the truth	Godliness
Believes all things, hopes all things	Knowledge
"Charity never faileth: but whether there be prophecies, they shall fail; whether there be tongues, they shall cease; whether there be knowledge, it shall vanish away."	"Wherefore the rather, brethren, give diligence to make your calling and election sure: for if ye do these things, ye shall never fall: for so an entrance shall be ministered unto you abundantly into the everlasting kingdom of our Lord and Savior Jesus Christ."

From this comparison we can see that charity is the composite of all the qualities Peter listed for our Christian life.

Love is the most important Christian virtue of all. Peter says, "And above all things have fervent charity among yourselves: for charity shall cover the multitude of sins" (1 Peter 4:8). And Paul echoes the idea, "Now the end of the commandment is charity out of a pure heart, and of a good conscience, and of faith unfeigned [sincere, genuine]" (1 Timothy 1:5).

Finally, Paul adds the simplest definition of all: "And above all these things put on charity, which is the bond of perfectness [completeness]" (Colossians 3:14). When we attain all the qualities Peter and Paul describe in these verses, the sum of them will be charity.

We have already examined how kindness is commanded of every Christian. Now we will add the intent of love that propels us to practice brotherly kindness. Paul tells us to walk charitably toward our weaker brothers (Romans 14:13–15). He also honored the Thessalonians because "the charity of every one of you all toward

PETER AND PAUL AGREED ON THE LOVE CHRISTIANS MUST DEVELOP.

each other aboundeth" (2 Thessalonians 1:3). John wrote to Christians: "Beloved, thou doest faithfully whatsoever thou doest to the brethren, and to strangers; which have borne witness of thy charity before the church" (3 John 1:5–6). In each of these passages, charity describes the love of Christians for others.

Charity—How Can I Develop It?

ex *Imitate the Father.* The best way to develop the kind of charity God expects us to have is to look at how He defines it. John tells us,

> He that loveth not knoweth not God; for God is love. In this was manifested the love of God toward us, because that God sent his only begotten Son into the world, that we might live through him (1 John 4:8–9).

Jesus came to earth as a sacrifice. His Father allowed it, and Jesus endured it. Our love, as much as possible, should be an imitation of the love He demonstrated. That is certainly easier said than done! We cannot ignore this fact—to imitate God's love, we must sacrifice. When His commands dictate kindness, godliness, patience, temperance, knowledge, virtue, and faith, why should we balk at sacrificing to develop these characteristics? We should expect to sacrifice in order to attain our abundant entrance into heaven!

∞ *Love one another.* John, the apostle of love, instructs us again on how to love one another. "This is my commandment, That ye love one another, as I [Jesus] have loved you" (John 15:12). God expects us to love each other in the same way He and Christ love us. Have you contemplated the seriousness of this commandment? When sisters have flaring tempers and engage in petty arguments, have they forgotten this plain truth? Jesus does not give us an option to love only the people that see everything just as we do. Read again about Gethsemane; then compare your love to that of our Lord. Take this command seriously, for by this love others know we belong to Christ.

∞ *Do everything in love.* Everything? That is what the Bible says, "Let all your things be done with charity" (1 Corinthians 16:14). That means we should consider our motives for all we do. Are our actions rooted in love? Think of your average day. Do you greet the day with love and thanksgiving? Do you incorporate deeds of service and kindness into your routine? Does this simple command go with you to the workplace, the grocery store, or to school? A Christian woman who takes inventory of her daily activities will find she has countless opportunities to ground her actions in love. Note that there are no exclusions to our attitude of love. The directive is for *all* things.

∞ *Love His Word, the Bible.* Our knowledge of, and love for God's Word must be the energy that powers our actions:

> If a man love me, he will keep my words: and my Father
> will love him, and we will come unto him, and make
> our abode with him. He that loveth me not keepeth not
> my sayings: and the word which ye hear is not mine,
> but the Father's which sent me (John 14:23–24).

God's Word is not like a popularity contest! It is the same—always. Culture does not change it. We show our love for God when we obey His Word. When a woman's behavior is contrary to God's law, the above verse teaches plainly that she does not love Him and He will not live in her. Many women have lost sight of God's standards in their struggle to fit in and be accepted by peers. But God's law is always in style. Don't you want Him to come and "make His abode" with you?

∞ *Love the gospel.* Christian women must love the good-news story of how Christ was born, lived, died, and was raised in our place. They must love it enough to tell it to others. "And this gospel of the kingdom shall be preached in all the world for a witness unto all nations; and then shall the end come" (Matthew 24:14). Do you have a strong belief that the gospel is true and can change our lives? Mark 1:15 states, "The time is fulfilled, and the kingdom of God is at hand: repent ye, and believe the gospel."

We must put the cause of the gospel before the needs of anything or anyone else.

> And Jesus answered and said, Verily I say unto you,
> There is no man that hath left house, or brethren, or
> sisters, or father, or mother, or wife, or children, or
> lands, for my sake, and the gospel's (Mark 10:29).

Finally, we must love the gospel enough to be willing to go and preach it to everyone everywhere, "Go ye into all the world, and preach the gospel to every creature" (Mark 16:15).

Adverse Side Effects of Having Charity

&ero; *Having charity in word only.* It's much easier to say you love someone than to show you love someone. Anyone striving to love God and love her fellowman the way God loves must make sure that the "saying" part of her love doesn't outweigh the "showing" part. John emphasizes this: "My little children, let us not love in word, neither with the tongue; but in deed and truth" (1 John 3:18).

&ero; *Having the wrong motives for loving others.* Another pitfall to watch for is appearing to have the wrong motive for your Christian love. Jesus condemned the Pharisees for wanting the praise of men. Paul also cautioned, "Whether therefore ye eat, or drink, or whatsoever ye do, do all to the glory of God" (1 Corinthians 10:31). The glory of God must be our objective in everything we do and say. Loving our fellowman must be powered by our love for God and our desire to bring glory to His name. No other motives are acceptable.

&ero; *Giving preferential treatment to some while others are in need.* Treating others equitably takes monumental effort. James reminds, "But if ye have respect to persons, ye commit sin, and are convinced of the law as transgressors" (James 2:9). Why is it so difficult to look beyond a person's dress, talent, or wealth and see her as a soul? Our tendency to gravitate only to people with like interests gets us in trouble with God's Word! How does a woman convince herself that showing partiality is sin? Just read the previous verse from James again. So often we excuse our behavior with "I'm only human." But the fact is, sin condemns; and it is a sin to have respect of persons. Maybe it is time for some soul searching. Jesus also emphasizes this principle of equitable treatment: "And as ye would that men should do to you, do ye also to them likewise" (Luke 6:31).

WOMEN OF CHARITY

Mary Magdalene

Mary Magdalene's fine example of charity is first mentioned by Luke.

> And it came to pass afterward, that he went throughout every city and village, preaching and shewing the glad tidings of the kingdom of God: and the twelve were with him, and certain women, which had been healed of evil spirits and infirmities, Mary called Magdalene, out of whom went seven devils, and Joanna the wife of Chuza Herod's steward, and Susanna, and many others, which ministered unto him of their substance (Luke 8:1–3).

Christ cleansed Mary of seven demons and she, along with other women, shared their assets with Christ and the disciples.

Mary is called Magdalene because she came from Magdala, a prosperous town on the coast of the Sea of Galilee about 120 miles north of Jerusalem. Magdala was known for its fish markets, dye works, and textile factories. "Magdalene" was probably added to her name to distinguish her from the other Marys who played a part in Jesus' life.

It is easy to conclude that Mary was financially comfortable, since she helped the other women who "ministered unto him [Christ] of their substance" (Luke 8:3). We don't know if she had ever been married, but it is reasonable to assume she was unmarried during the time of Christ's ministry, because she and others followed Him as He preached and taught.

Not a Prostitute

For almost two thousand years, Mary Magdalene has been accused of being a prostitute. The Bible does not teach that! Pope Gregory, a sixth-century head of the Roman church, declared that Mary Magdalene, Mary of Bethany, and the sinful women spoken of in Luke 7:36–50 were the same person—a forgiven prostitute.

Mary of Bethany might have been the sinful woman who anointed Christ's feet and dried them with their hair, but nowhere do we find that Mary Magdalene was a prostitute. Regardless of her previous life, Mary Magdalene was totally committed to Christ. She had close contact with Joanna, the wife of Chuza, Herod's steward, and Susanna (Luke 8:3), as well as Mary, the mother of James the Less, Joses, and Salome (Mark 15:40). She was also in the company of the mother of the sons of Zebedee, Jesus' mother, and His mother's sister Mary, the wife of Clopas. (See Matthew 27:56 and John 19:25.)

Mary Magdalene demonstrated her total commitment to Christ. She followed His directions when He said,

> Whosoever will come after me, let him deny himself, and take up his cross, and follow me. For whosoever will save his life will lose it, but whosoever shall lose his life for my sake and the gospel's, the same shall save it (Mark 8:34–35).

What Did She Do?

Mary Magdalene's charity had several facets.

ఴ *She left her home in Galilee to follow Christ.*

> And many women were there beholding afar off, which followed Jesus from Galilee, ministering unto him: among which was Mary Magdalene, and Mary the mother of James and Joses, and the mother of Zebedee's children (Matthew 27:55–56).

℘ *She and the other women cared for Jesus.* The Bible says they "ministered unto Him." That means they attended His physical wants and needs. Mary Magdalene almost certainly shared her supplies and money with Christ and the disciples.

℘ *She was with Christ to offer support when He preached.* Mary Magdalene showed her Christian charity by following Christ's teaching schedule. Sometimes a friend's presence means more than anything money can buy.

℘ *She stayed with Christ through the hardest of times—His crucifixion.* All four writers of the Gospels tell about her presence there (Mark 15:40; Luke 23:49; John 19:25).

℘ *She witnessed Christ's death.* She was present when Joseph wrapped His body and placed it in his personal tomb. Matthew 27:61 says, "And there was Mary Magdalene, and the other Mary, sitting over against the sepulcher."

℘ *She saw the empty tomb.* After the Sabbath, she and another Mary went to the tomb to anoint Christ's body with more spices.

> In the end of the sabbath, as it began to dawn toward the first day of the week, came Mary Magdalene and the other Mary to see the sepulcher. And, behold, there was a great earthquake: for the angel of the Lord descended from heaven, and came and rolled back the stone from the door, and sat upon it. His countenance was like lightning, and his raiment white as snow: and for fear of him the keepers did shake, and became as dead men. And the angel answered and said unto the women, Fear not ye: for I know that ye seek Jesus, which was crucified. He is not here: for he is risen (Matthew 28:1–6).

ൟ *She saw the risen Savior.* Matthew 28:9 records, "And as [Mary Magdalene and the other Mary] went to tell his disciples, behold, Jesus met them, saying, All hail. And they came and held him by the feet, and worshipped him."

ൟ *She spoke to the risen Christ.* John 20:16 says, "Jesus saith unto her, Mary. She turned herself, and saith unto him, Rabboni; which is to say, Master."

ൟ *She was the first person to announce Christ's triumph over death.* John 20:18 continues, "Mary Magdalene came and told the disciples that she had seen the Lord, and that he had spoken these things unto her."

Through Mary Magdalene's actions we can understand that charity involves much more than giving at the office or donating loose change to a worthy cause. The true Christian charity Peter prescribes is a lifestyle of giving of your means and yourself. Anything less is unacceptable to God.

QUESTIONS ABOUT YOUR PRESCRIPTION

1. What is charity?

2. What is the difference between charity and the other kinds of love?

3. Do you believe that charity is the most important Christian virtue? Why or why not?

4. Do most people understand the meaning of charity as used by Peter? Suggest ways to help those who do not.

5. Share some of the speculations you have heard about Mary Magdalene. Are they true or false? Defend your answer.

6. What should be the mindset of a Christian who does a charitable deed for another person?

7. If we have any misunderstandings about the definition of charity, where should we look to find answers to our questions?

8. Do you believe the giver of a charitable gift should always get some kind of thanks or gratitude? Why or why not?

9. Discuss other women in the Bible who had charitable natures.

10. What does Peter say our reward will be if we add all the qualities in his prescription to our Christian character?

FURTHER RESEARCH

෨ Describe an instance of outstanding charity you've witnessed in the last year.

෨ Compare "respect of persons" and agape love.

Abundance

THE DIVINE DIAGNOSIS

PRESCRIPTION

For if these things be in you, and abound, they make you that ye shall neither be barren nor unfruitful . . . But he that lacketh these things is blind, and cannot see afar off, and hath forgotten that he was purged from his old sins. Wherefore . . . give diligence to make your calling and election sure: for if ye do these things, ye shall never fall: For so an entrance shall be ministered unto you abundantly *into the everlasting kingdom of our Lord and Savior Jesus Christ* (2 Peter 1:8–11).

PHYSICIAN'S INSTRUCTIONS

Search me, O God, and know my heart: try me, and know my thoughts: And see if there be any wicked way in me, and lead me in the way everlasting (Psalm 139:23–24).

DAILY DOSE

Mark 11:12–14   Mark 11:21–22
Colossians 1:9–10   1 Peter 4:18

What Is Abundance?

Abundance is "a fullness of spirit that overflows, a more than plentiful quantity of something."

"For if these things be in you, and abound, they make you that ye shall neither be barren nor unfruitful in the knowledge of our Lord Jesus Christ." This passage refers to the Christian graces Peter listed in verses 5–7. If a Christian has a full measure of each quality—faith, virtue, knowledge, temperance, patience, godliness, brotherly kindness, and charity—she will have no reason not to bear fruit for the Lord. Fruitfulness refers to teaching others about Christ.

To use our physician analogy once more, think of a special diet that your doctor might prescribe for an illness. Similarly, think of the Christian qualities we've discussed as types of foods for Christians' souls. These foods strengthen us and make us more enthusiastic about Christ and His church. Peter is observing that a diet of these kinds of "foods" will undoubtedly make each Christian stronger and more able to bring others to Christ.

Paul also refers to Christians bearing fruit:

> For this cause we also, since the day we heard it, do not cease to pray for you, and to desire that ye might be filled with the knowledge of his will in all wisdom and spiritual understanding; that ye might walk worthy of the Lord unto all pleasing, being fruitful in every good work, and increasing in the knowledge of God (Colossians 1:9–10).

We can rest assured that God will recognize our good works because He prepares us to do them.

> All scripture is given by inspiration of God, and is profitable for doctrine, for reproof, for correction, for instruction in righteousness: That the man of God may be perfect, thoroughly furnished unto all good works (2 Timothy 3:16–17).

What can our souls possibly need that the Scripture does not supply? It is a deep well of strength and instruction.

The "Prescription" continues with these words: "But he that lacketh these things is blind, and cannot see afar off, and hath forgotten that he was purged from his old sins." Again, Peter uses a physical comparison when he says that a Christian who does not have a complete supply of these "foods" may think that she can see, when in reality, she is blind. She can't "see afar off" and doesn't remember the kind of person she was before God forgave her sins. We can "put on a holy face" for our friends and fellow church members, but if we lack the Christian qualities in 2 Peter, in reality, we are weak and blind.

Positive and Negative Views

Verses 9–10 describe two sides of the same issue. On the positive side, "ye shall neither be barren nor unfruitful in the knowledge of our Lord Jesus Christ" if you possess and put to work the seven qualities we have studied. However, verse 9 shows us the negative side of the issue by saying, "But he that lacketh these things is blind, and cannot see afar off, and hath forgotten that he was purged from his old sins."

> WE CAN "PUT ON A HOLY FACE" AND YET BE WEAK AND BLIND.

Christians with strong, rich, full characters who produce other Christians through good works and love are on one side of the field. On the other side are Christians with stunted spiritual growth, void of these characteristics. They are blind and forgetful of their previous state and the gift of salvation God gave them. Who do you think will win the victory?

Peter is absolutely sure who will win because he says, "Wherefore the rather, brethren, give diligence to make your calling and election sure: for if ye do these things, ye shall never fall" (2 Peter 1:10). He instructs us to be diligent—constant in an effort to accomplish our goals. We can't let up; we must work every day to make our calling and election sure. This is where Dr. Peter becomes our cheerleader and coach. He's saying, "Don't stop! Practice these virtues every day and you'll show that you're champions and winners!"

"If" and "Never Fall"

Peter goes on to say that we will never fall if we continue to do the Lord's will. Think of a baby who is learning to walk. She is full of confidence and purpose so long as she is being supported by someone. Likewise, we can be brave because we know our Lord is supporting our efforts, "for *if* ye do these things, ye shall *never fall*" (2 Peter 1:10). We cannot accept the "never fall" of this verse without the "if." The baby who is learning to walk gains confidence, in spite of her stumbling. She goes through many "ifs" before learning how not to fall! We are our Father's children, even as adults. Peter gives prescriptions for never falling, but the "if" is our responsibility.

The passage concludes with Peter's announcing what our prize for this contest will be: "For so an entrance shall be ministered unto you abundantly into the everlasting kingdom of our Lord and Savior Jesus Christ." Our welcome to heaven will be abundant and elaborate. It will be fantastic to be welcomed into a place we have longed to reach. Matthew describes a Christian's homecoming in heaven like this: "Then shall the King say unto them on his right hand, Come, ye blessed of my Father, inherit the kingdom prepared for you from the foundation of the world" (Matthew 25:34).

Paul also discusses the Judgment Day and our entrance into the presence of our Lord: "For we must all appear before the judgment seat of Christ, that each one may be recompensed for his deeds in the body, according to what he has done, whether good or bad" (2 Corinthians 5:10). If we have followed Peter's prescription and have added all the qualities to our characters, we can be confident and look forward to the judgment.

We must be constantly reminding ourselves of this goal and continually making an effort to achieve it. Perhaps, by remembering some examples of the Christians qualities with which we can strengthen our souls, we can ensure that others will reach the goal with us. Our "fruit" will be the other Christians in heaven whom we have taught about our Lord.

How Can I Abound in the Lord?

So here we are. We have been diagnosed, received the prescription, studied the ingredients, and know what our desired outcome should be. What's our next step?

Growing or abounding in the Lord, is a process, not an event. Perhaps you have completed this study and are not sure what to do next. If you haven't been added to the Lord's church through baptism, your first task should be to go to a Christian you know and trust and ask for assistance in reading God's roadmap to salvation. If you've finished this book as part of a Bible class study, ask the teacher or another classmate to help you. If you have studied alone, call the nearest congregation of the Lord's church and talk to the preacher or one of the elders. In either case, prepare yourself for the most wonderful and amazing gift you will ever receive by reading and studying these scriptures that clearly instruct you how to be saved:

God's Gift of Salvation	
Romans 10:17	Hear God's Word.
Hebrews 11:6; John 8:24	Believe in Jesus Christ.
Luke 13:3; Acts 2:38; Acts 3:19	Repent of your sins.
Matthew 10:32; Romans 10:9–10	Confess that Jesus is the Son of God.
Mark 16:16; Acts 2:38	Be baptized.
2 Peter 1:10; Romans 12:1	Live faithfully unto death.

If you have been baptized for the remission of your sins, your next step in abounding in the Lord might be a personal inventory of how many of Peter's prescriptions you are taking. Are you practicing the qualities Peter prescribed for all Christians? You may wish to use the survey below or develop your own way of measuring your progress. Just keep in mind that you should be honest with yourself: this process is personal and entirely private.

"If These Be in You and Abound . . ."

1. I consciously try to strengthen my faith:
   __ Always __ Very Often __ Sometimes __ Rarely __ Never

2. I practice virtue in my daily life:
   __ Always __ Very Often __ Sometimes __ Rarely __ Never

3. I add daily to my knowledge of God's Word:
   __ Always __ Very Often __ Sometimes __ Rarely __ Never

4. I practice temperance in my daily life:
   __ Always __ Very Often __ Sometimes __ Rarely __ Never

5. I am patient:
   __ Always __ Very Often __ Sometimes __ Rarely __ Never

6. I try to show godliness in all my actions:
   __ Always __ Very Often __ Sometimes __ Rarely __ Never

7. My actions show with brotherly kindness:
   __ Always __ Very Often __ Sometimes __ Rarely __ Never

8. Charity (or love) guides my thinking and actions:
   __ Always __ Very Often __ Sometimes __ Rarely __ Never

9. I abound in the qualities Peter prescribed for Christians:
   __ Always __ Very Often __ Sometimes __ Rarely __ Never

PERFECT EXAMPLE OF ABUNDANCE

Jesus of Nazareth—the Great Physician

1. *Faith*—We do not often discuss the faith of Jesus in our daily Bible studies. But Jesus had faith in His Father, just as we are to have faith in Him (Jesus). Several scriptures support this statement. Paul writes,

   > I am crucified with Christ: nevertheless I live; yet not I, but Christ liveth in me: and the life which I now live in the flesh I live by the faith of the Son of God, who loved me, and gave himself for me (Galatians 2:20).

   Here Paul is saying that the faith Jesus had and showed in His willingness to go to the cross for our sins supports Paul and enables him to live a life free from sin. Jesus completes our faith by taking up our cause when we are unable to continue. In Mark 9:24, the father who had come to Jesus to help his child says with tears: "Lord, I believe; help thou mine unbelief." Christ's faith enables us to achieve maturity. "And ye are complete in him, which is the head of all principality and power" (Colossians 2:10).

2. *Virtue*—If anyone has ever led a virtuous life, Jesus surely did. Of course, we recognize that His supernatural side supported and encouraged Him in His actions. He had angels to comfort Him after He had endured the wiles of the devil. "Then the devil leaveth him, and, behold, angels came and ministered unto him" (Matthew 4:11). But the virtue He showed as He lived here on earth was born of His human desire to do good, He "went about doing good, and healing all that were oppressed of the devil" (Acts 10:38).

- *Jesus was virtuous because of His knowledge of God's Word.* Jesus often quoted the Old Testament. It is obvious that He had studied it and committed it to memory. He rebuffed the devil by quoting Scripture: "Man shall not live by bread alone" (Deuteronomy 8:3; Matthew 4:4). "Thou shalt not tempt the Lord thy God" (Deuteronomy 6:16; Matthew 4:7). "Thou shalt worship the Lord thy God, and him only shalt thou serve" (Deuteronomy 6:13; Matthew 4:10).

- *Jesus was virtuous because of the way He prayed.* Jesus prayed because He needed to talk to God in private. "And in the morning, rising up a great while before day, he went out, and departed into a solitary place, and there prayed" (Mark 1:35).

- *Jesus prayed for His friends.* "Simon, Simon, behold, Satan hath desired to have you, that he may sift you as wheat: but I have prayed for thee, that thy faith fail not: and when thou art converted, strengthen thy brethren" (Luke 22:31–32).

- *Jesus prayed for Himself.* "And being in an agony he prayed more earnestly: and his sweat was as it were great drops of blood falling down to the ground" (Luke 22:44).

- *Jesus prayed as an example for others.* "And Jesus lifted up his eyes, and said, Father, I thank thee that thou hast heard me. And I knew that thou hearest me always: but because of the people which stand by I said it, that they may believe that thou hast sent me" (John 11:41–42).

3. *Knowledge*—As Jesus lived as a man on earth, He gained knowledge both intellectually and socially. "And Jesus increased in wisdom and stature, and in favor with God

and man" (Luke 2:52). In His humanity, he became an example to all men. God had previously told Hosea, "My people are destroyed for lack of knowledge: because thou hast rejected knowledge" (Hosea 4:6). Therefore, we know that Jesus desired to gain knowledge in order to please His Father. He studied the Scriptures and quoted them often. Isaiah prophesied that Christ would be filled with knowledge:

> And the spirit of the Lord shall rest upon him, the spirit of wisdom and understanding, the spirit of counsel and might, the spirit of knowledge and of the fear of the Lord; and shall make him of quick understanding in the fear of the Lord: and he shall not judge after the sight of his eyes, neither reprove after the hearing of his ears (Isaiah 11:2–3).

4. *Temperance*—Jesus was our foremost example of temperance: He withstood priests, kings, and even Satan, and remained calm and in control of Himself and the situation. He was the very picture of moderation and self-restraint (1 Peter 2:23). Through His temperance and moderation, Jesus was sinless in His life: "For such an high priest became us, who is holy, harmless, undefiled, separate from sinners, and made higher than the heavens" (Hebrews 7:26). Even at the point of death, the temperate nature of Jesus prevailed and He had no sin of His own, "For he hath made him to be sin for us, who knew no sin; that we might be made the righteousness of God in him" (2 Corinthians 5:21).

5. *Patience*—The entire earthly life of Jesus was one of patience and longsuffering. Even though He was equal to God, Jesus patiently lived within the restrictions of His humanity for thirty-three years on this earth:

Characteristics of His Humanity	Scriptures
1. Born to human parents	Matthew 1, Mark 3, Luke 2, John 2
2. Was a baby	Luke 2:12, 16
3. Was a child	Matthew 2, Luke 2
4. Was a boy	Luke 2:43
5. Called a man	Matthew 8:27; Mark 2:7
6. Had human brothers & sisters	Matthew 12:47; Mark 3:31; Luke 8:19
7. Had a body	Luke 23:52; John 1:14; Colossians 1:22
8. Had a soul	Matthew 26:38; John12:27
9. Had a spirit	Mark 2:8
10. Became hungry	Matthew 4:2; 21:18; Mark 11:12
11. Ate food	Matthew 11:19; Mark 14:22; Luke 7:34
12. Became tired	John 4:6
13. Became thirsty	John 4:7
14. Drank liquids	Matthew 11:19
15. Tried to escape the crowds	Luke 4:42
16. Wept	John 11:35

Just imagine the amount of patience it took for Jesus to endure the day-to-day struggles of life! The Bible tells us that He could have employed heavenly forces to protect Him from those who came to imprison Him: "Thinkest thou that I cannot now pray to my Father, and he shall presently give me more than twelve legions of angels?" (Matthew 26:53.) But He didn't. He patiently waited for the Scriptures to be fulfilled.

6. *Godliness*—No one has ever exhibited more godliness than Jesus Christ did. Paul tells us how the great mystery of Jesus' godliness occurred,

> And without controversy great is the mystery of godliness: God was manifest in the flesh, justified in the Spirit, seen of angels, preached unto the Gentiles,

believed on in the world, received up into glory (1 Timothy 3:16).

Everything Jesus said and did was pleasing to God (Matthew 3:17). Jesus desired to be godly and to please His heavenly Father (John 8:29). Jesus made sure that we have everything we need to live godly lives, and He knew that godliness was good for us. He had Paul to say, "But godliness with contentment is great gain" (1 Timothy 6:6).

7. *Brotherly kindness*—Jesus Christ was our perfect example and teacher concerning brotherly kindness. Jesus told us to possess brotherly kindness: "My command is this: Love each other as I have loved you. Greater love has no one than this, that he lay down his life for his friends" (John 15:12–13). Jesus wanted brotherly kindness to grow among Christians: "Let brotherly love continue" (Hebrews 13:1). And Jesus knew that brotherly kindness makes our hearts pure: "Seeing ye have purified your souls in obeying the truth through the Spirit unto unfeigned love of the brethren, see that ye love one another with a pure heart fervently" (1 Peter 1:22).

8. *Charity*—Jesus is our best guide and pattern as we seek to show charity and love to our fellow Christians. Jesus loved sinners (Mark 10:21). Jesus loved his friends, (John 11:35). Jesus loved all those who followed Him (John 13:1). Nothing can separate us from the love of Jesus and God: "Nor height, nor depth, nor any other creature, shall be able to separate us from the love of God, which is in Christ Jesus our Lord" (Romans 8:39).

And finally, all Christians need to have charity in order to be saved. "And above all things have fervent charity among yourselves: for charity shall cover the multitude of sins" (1 Peter 4:8).

We had the following objectives for this study:

ౚ Define each quality that the writer lists.

ౚ Search the Bible to find out how we can acquire each characteristic.

ౚ Examine the lives of women in the Bible who possessed each attribute.

It is my sincerest hope and prayer that you have achieved these goals in your study of *Prescriptions for a Woman's Soul*. If it were possible to summarize 2 Peter 1: 5–11 in a sentence, I would ask that you keep in mind what Christ said to his followers: "And as ye would that men should do to you, do ye also to them likewise" (Luke 6:31) and put it into action in your daily life. True Christian growth is achieved one step at a time, one word at a time, and one good deed at a time. Do not become discouraged or impatient with yourself as long as you are making a continuous, conscious effort to study and follow the teachings of Christ. May God bless and keep you all.

QUESTIONS ABOUT YOUR PRESCRIPTION

1. What does being fruitful mean to a Christian?

2. Are those directly involved in teaching and baptizing sinners the only Christians who can be considered fruitful? Why or why not?

3. What are some activities that contribute to fruitfulness? How is teaching small children one of these activities?

4. How are Christians "called" today?

5. How can a Christian stay-at-home mom bear fruit?

6. What kind of heavenly welcome will a fruitful Christian receive?

7. Why do Christians get discouraged when they don't develop these qualities quickly?

8. What is the one tool every Christian needs as she strives to become fruitful and obedient?

9. List some of your goals for living a Christian life.